For They Shall See God

Developing a Transformed Vision

by

David Beck

Foreword by

Archbishop Nathaniel of Detroit

© 2017 Theosis Books

www.theosisbooks.net

Cover photos by Joelle Paur

Nature photo by Christina Beck

ISBN 9781541149519
Printed in the United States of America.

Acknowledgments

Over the years, I have been blessed by many "signposts" who have pointed me to the Orthodox Church. Two of my mentors have left this world: Dr. Charles Ashanin and Fr. Nathaniel Eichner. May their memory be eternal! They along with Brian McDonald and Fr. John Schmidt served as guides for my entrance into the Church. The counsel and wisdom of Archimandrite Joseph (Morris) helped me to grow in my understanding of Church life and my vocation within her.

Thanks to Marty Nagy whose friendship has inspired many great conversations that shaped my approach not just to writing, but to life in general. Further, his editorial comments and suggestions made this book much stronger. I greatly appreciate his hard work to finish editing this project during a very busy time in his life.

I am grateful as well to the love and support from Fr. David Wey and the community of Sts. Constantine and Elena Orthodox Church of which I am a member.

Thank you to Theodore Nottingham for his willingness to put *For They Shall See God* back in print through Theosis Books.

Last and certainly not least, I am grateful for the love and encouragement I undeservedly receive from Susie, my wife, and my son, Michael and my daughter, Christina.

Blessed are the poor in heart, for they shall see God.

-Matt. 5:8

When thou seest thy brother, thou seest God.

-Clement of Alexandria

(*Stomatis*, I, 19, 94)

Raise up the stone, and thou shall find Me; cleave the tree and I am there.

-*Oxyrhynchus Logia*

Table of Contents

Foreword...7

Introduction...13

1 Toward a Transformed Vision....................17

2 The Human Person as Image and Likeness......33

3 The Mystical Vision: Seeing Beyond the Veil....55

4 The Path to Purity................................85

5 The Dance.......................................141

Bibliography..159

For They Shall See God

Foreword

by Archbishop Nathaniel

Orthodox Christianity, the Body of Christ founded in Jerusalem on Pentecost, at home in the Middle East and Africa, and found in various expressions in Europe, is best known in North America due to the presence of the existence of numbers of "ethnic" American Orthodox who continue to bear witness to the faith of their fathers.

In recent decades the beliefs of the Orthodox have come to be known because of the proliferation of English language books published on the subject and to a more active personal and public witness.

The reasons for the existence of these English publications are varied. One is that younger generations of believers no longer speak the ethnic tongue of their forbearers. Living as Americans, inter-marrying with people of various ethnic backgrounds and of different faiths, they have insisted on having English books to satisfy their need to "know" their faith.

Another reason is that there is a growing number of non-Orthodox who have become curious about the Church and who, at their own initiative, sat down and translated works of interest.

We must not neglect to state and be thankful that a growing number of American theologians, clerical and lay, have had their own original works published.

Among these are books written about various "Orthodox spiritualties" i.e. Arab, Greek, Russian and Slavic. These works speak of the beauty of the various and unique ethnic expressions of the faith. We must remember, however, that there is no essential theological difference between these various expressions of Orthodoxy. They all affirm the truth that, working with and through such national identities, is the Holy Spirit who upholds the unity of faith and the fellowship of the saints in the One, Holy, Catholic and Apostolic Church.

Through his book, *For They Shall See God*, David Beck gives to American Orthodox and to the seeker, an original work, a wonderful guide, a fresh witness. For his topic, he has chosen to consider one of the most profound questions, "Can God be known, and if so, who can see Him?"

Basing our journey toward seeing God on the affirmation that God does reveal himself, we continue along the way to come to experience the Almighty. We are directed toward the path to follow in our lives, fulfilling, perfecting, and transforming ourselves, through communion in the Church, into the full likeness of the Creator whose image we bear from conception.

"You cannot see my face; for man shall not see me and live" (Ex. 33:20), says the Lord to Moses, but "Blessed are the pure in heart, for they shall see God" (Matt. 5:8), promises the Lord Jesus to the crowds. Exploring the meaning of these two seemingly opposing Scriptural texts, Beck guides us to the reality of a "Transformed Vision," a vision such as was experienced by the apostles on Mount Tabor.

Using Sacred Scripture, the writings of the Holy Fathers and the Saints, along with writings of Christian authors of our own day, Beck walks us through the refreshing statements of faith and the experiences of those who have, "crossed over from the flesh to the spirit." He leads us, as it were, to the well of Samaria into which we are invited to dip our souls to quench the thirst of our own quest to "see" God.

Many "Christians" today, among whom there are also some "Orthodox," challenge something which David Beck reaffirms as essential for the believer, that " ... our spiritual growth is dependent upon our life in the Church. It is through the Church that the Holy Spirit transforms us into the likeness of God."

To be a Christian, a believer, is also to be disciplined. St. Paul uses images of athletes, soldiers and others who discipline themselves to fulfill their goals, to teach the faithful that knowledge of God and of the inner vision is not a haphazard reward but the fruit of "synergy," a gift of co-working with the Holy Spirit.

The tools of the Christian are fasting, prayer and almsgiving, instruments which, in some circles have become blunt, lying neglected in the tool box of spiritual exercise, while others have cast them away as futile remnants of a by-gone era. Beck's is a useful reminder to sharpen those tools and use them.

For They Shall See God will become a popular book
for it speaks clearly and directly. It is the result of
personal study, reflection and experience. Although the
topic itself is profound, the book is not bogged down in
terminology too frightening or abstract for us to
comprehend. Although it is a book about a profound
subject, nevertheless, because it is readable for all levels of
the faithful, it will have a wide circulation. Most of all,
however, it satisfies a thirst for the knowledge contained
therein.

It can be stated with assurance that this welcome
volume, once read, will not collect dust on the shelf but
will become a part of the reader's discipline and continue
to share the meditative life. It can be used as a "prayer"
book, as a reference volume and, assuredly as a catechism.

For They Shall See God is a well-spring into which
one can dip, and dip, and dip again, for refreshment along
life's journey "to see God." We are grateful to David
Beck, for his work and look forward to future
publications to enrich the library of English works on the
Orthodox Faith. In the meantime, delay no longer. Take

up this volume and begin the journey to purifying our hearts, so that we, too, may see God.

NATHANIEL

Bishop of Detroit

Romanian Episcopate

Feast of the Presentation 1995

Introduction

This book was conceived after attending a study on the Beatitudes, based on the interpretations of St. Gregory of Nyssa. The longer I reflected on the idea of seeing God in ourselves, others, and nature, the more I discovered similar teachings in the writings of other saints and theologians. I wrote an article on this subject, but as time went by I saw the need to expand these ideas into this book.

The writing has challenged me for several reasons. First, I am not a theologian in the technical sense, and the theological beliefs of the first two chapters were gleaned from several sources. Second, I am no monk or mystic, so the practices conveyed in the final three chapters I gleaned from those far more experienced in the Christian life than I. Like many others, these experiences have occurred from time to time, when it is as if our eyes are seeing beyond the surface and penetrating the mystery of existence, but never on a regular basis.

Knowing my limitations and lack of mystical experiences, I questioned whether I could adequately present the experiences and practices of others, experiences and practices that I myself find difficult to attain, let alone maintain. Christian literature has many wonderful and inspiring accounts, accounts that nonetheless often seem foreign to our everyday lives. My firm conviction is that the Orthodox faith is practical and down-to-earth. Those teachers of the faith, then, who inspire us to walk more closely with God and increase our thirst for Him, offer invaluable practical guidance for our everyday Christian life. If it is not practical, then it is of little use. Jesus Christ was a real man as well as being God Himself. He walked, talked, ate, and suffered while on earth. His teachings were practical and were handed down not to scholars or esoteric individuals but to men and women who were planted firmly on the ground, who worked, laughed, and loved with the common people who surrounded them. Hence, if the mystical teaching of the Church is true, and I believe it is, it must transform our lives in a real and practical way. Our love for God and our neighbor should deepen. We should be obedient to Him, no matter in what circumstances we find ourselves.

My hope is that this book might help inspire the reader to live a more single-minded life, a life with all its complexities, nuances, and confusion can be turned over to God, at each and every moment. Many of the examples and teachings have been gathered from the lives of those far more experienced in the spiritual life than I am; but we must accept their lives and teachings as the "ideal." They inspire us by showing what the "divinized" life is like. Our goal should be to follow their examples as closely as possible, always remembering that such a life is filled with struggle. In return we experience the Kingdom of God in our daily lives, even if we can only catch glimpses of God working in us, through us, and around us. My belief, and the point of this book, is that as our hearts are purified and we become more single-minded our vision will be transformed and we will see God's image in ourselves and others and His imprint upon all creation. Then, we will not only realize but experience the Kingdom of God in us and around us.

Regarding citations, I have tried to footnote most of the sources; however, I often write quotes on scraps of paper or cards without mentioning the source. Also, all Scriptural references are from the Revised Standard Version, unless noted otherwise.

1

Toward a Transformed Vision

One of the most interesting, encouraging, and yet puzzling statements in the Beatitudes is "Blessed are the pure in heart, for they shall see God" (Matt 5:8). These words of Christ have a more mystical character than any of the other Beatitudes. Moreover, they seem to contradict what the Lord told Moses: "You cannot see my face; for man shall not see me and live" (Ex 33:20). Even in the Gospel of John we find: "No one has seen God" (Jn 1:18), except through the Son.

What is Jesus telling us? One might understand this verse as being solely eschatological, seeing it as pertaining only to the future kingdom to come. Such an understanding is correct, but incomplete. Many of the Church Fathers saw the verse as having a two-fold meaning: the first is eschatological referring to the future Kingdom; the second, however, refers to the present, to the Kingdom at hand.

If it is possible to "see" God in the present, how do we reconcile this possibility with those scriptural passages that seem to contradict such an experience? Several refer to "seeing" God in the future kingdom. For example, we find in St. John's first epistle, "Beloved, we are God's children now; it does not yet appear what we shall be, but we know that when he appears we shall be like him, for we shall see him as he is" (I Jn 3:2). Later he writes, "No man has ever seen God; if we love one another, God abides in us and his love is perfected in us" (I Jn 4:12). In St. Paul's first epistle to Timothy, God is described as the "Lord of lords, who alone has immortality and dwells in unapproachable light, whom no man has ever seen or can see" (I Tim 6:16).

Yet we find instances in the Old Testament of those who have seen God in some form. Isaiah cried, "Woe is me! For I am lost; for I am a man of unclean lips, and I dwell in the midst of a people of unclean lips; for my eyes have seen the King, the Lord of hosts!" (Isa 6:5). These manifestations of God, or theophanies, are usually interpreted as God revealing Himself in a tangible form while concealing his true essence, which is unknowable, let alone something visible. Such a view would explain how God could wrestle with Jacob (Gen 32: 22-30). After his encounter, Jacob proclaimed: "I have seen God face to face, and yet my life is preserved" (Gen 32:30). Whether Jacob actually wrestled with a manifestation of God or an angel is unclear. In another example, Manoah and his wife saw an angel of the Lord. Manoah cried, "We shall surely die, for we have seen God" (Judg 13:22). This scriptural tension between beholding and not looking at God is depicted in those icons of the Nativity where Mary is looking away from Jesus, for He is God and cannot be looked upon. Yet we know, as His Mother, she often looked at Him.

These Old Testament passages, and others like them, have been interpreted in many ways. Yet the consensus of the Holy Fathers and the teaching of the Church remains: that God, in His essence, is beyond our visual capacity. At times He has manifested Himself in ways that can be seen. The clearest example is found, of course, in the Incarnation. These theophanies, however, are uncommon. Further, they have little to do with Christ's statement, "Blessed are the pure in heart, for they shall see God" (Matt 5:8).

The Fathers also taught that the promise of this Beatitude refers to the present, preceding the time when we shall see Him "face to face" (I Cor 13:12). But if it is true that, as many of the Fathers taught, we can see God in the present, how is it possible? If the criterion is "purity of heart," what does it mean to be pure of heart and how is it attained? Moreover, what does such a transformation mean for our personal lives as well as for the life of our parishes?

Another more immediate question comes to mind: Is this transformation available to all Christians or just ascetic men and women living in monasteries or in solitude? St. Symeon the New Theologian believed such an experience is available to us all:

Do not say that God does not manifest Himself to
    man.

Do not say that men cannot perceive the divine light, or that it is impossible in this age!

Never is it found to be impossible, my friends. On the contrary it is entirely possible when one desires it.[1]

It should be added, too, that this transformation, which we shall explore, is not an either/or proposition. It is better described as "degrees" than whether one can or cannot see God. The ability to see God in our daily lives is a gift, a gift that is not received, however, without effort and struggle. Our everyday situations, then, do affect our spirituality but do not exclude us completely from having our vision transformed.

Before discussing "purity of heart," let us examine the patristic and scriptural understanding of the heart. Writers and the Church Fathers considered the heart to be the center of a person's being. It is the seed of our thoughts and our will. Within the heart we find our "entire mental and moral activity."[2] It is both the center of physical life as well of our moral and spiritual life.[3] Through the cleansing of our heart our inner vision is transformed.

What then does it mean to be "pure in heart"? The Greek word for "pure," *katharos*, means to be cleansed or chaste.[4] To be cleansed is an act of God (Ps 51:10) and is also a part of our own struggle to gain victory over the passions. In other words, becoming "pure in heart" is a synergistic act. For the New Testament writers and the Church Fathers, becoming pure in heart requires both the work of God and the work of the Christian. The result is a heart that is "single-minded," focused completely on the will of God. It would not be wrong to say that being pure in heart means having "one intention," that intention being God Himself.

Thomas Merton had a good understanding of the Eastern Christian perspective of purity of heart. He writes,

> [Natural contemplation] is the intuition of divine things in and through the reflection of God in nature and in the symbols of revelation. It presupposes a complete purification of heart by a long ascetic preparation which has delivered the soul from subjection to passion and, consequently, from the illusions generated by passionate attachment to exterior things. When the eye is clear and "single" (that is to say

disinterested—having only one intention) then it can see things as they are.[5]

In other words, when we see things *as they are*, we see the divine; we see God! This vision is not of His essence (which we will differentiate later) but of His image as it is stamped through all creation, and most perfectly in the human person. Through personal asceticism and through the grace of God, our vision is transformed.

God's glory is manifested in all creation. But it is only through the purifying of our hearts that we are able to see all of creation as it truly is: a reflection of God's image. (In the case of some people, especially the saints, we see also the *likeness* of God.) St. Gregory of Nyssa teaches that "the evil that has been poured all around the nature bearing the Divine Image has rendered useless to you this wonderful thing that lies hidden under vile coverings. If, therefore, you wash off by a good life the filth that has been stuck on your heart like plaster, the Divine Beauty will again shine forth in you."[6] Fr. Thomas Hopko writes, "The pure in heart see God everywhere—in themselves, in others, in everyone and everything. They know that the 'heavens declare the glory of God and the earth shows forth the work of his hands' (Ps 19:1)."[7]

For the pure in heart the image of God can be seen in all created things. In the human person, however, we are able to see the image *and*, to greater and lesser degrees, the likeness of God. At the same time, we can, through purification and God's grace, grow in the likeness of God.

It should be clear by now that when we talk about "seeing" God, we are not referring to some profound visual experience of divine light (though as we have seen in the lives of the saints, this is possible). It is instead a transformation of our "inner eye," seeing God through his imprint and image in all of creation. This vision is progressive and usually does not come at once. It is not a state at which one arrives, never to lose his or her sight again. We as Christians prepare our hearts through purification but must wait ultimately on God to open our eyes, whenever He chooses.

To find an example of such a visual transformation we must look no further than the Transfiguration of our

Lord. This event has been interpreted by the Fathers as occurring because the disciples' eyes were opened, not because the Lord momentarily changed. St. Gregory Palamas states that

> the transformation of our human nature, its deification and transfiguration—were these not accomplished in Christ from the start, from the moment in which He assumed our nature? Thus He was divine before, but He bestowed at the time of His Transfiguration a divine power upon the eyes of the apostles and enabled them to look up and see for themselves.[8]

Palamas corroborates his argument by quoting St. John of Damascus: "Christ is transfigured, not by putting on some quality He did not possess previously, nor by changing into something He never was before, but by revealing to His disciples what He truly was, in opening their eyes and in giving sight to those who were blind."[9] Thus, Christ is not changed into something new; instead His disciples are able to see His true glory, which is revealed when their eyes see beyond the veil of His flesh that He took upon himself in the Incarnation.

St. Maximum the Confessor described this transformation. He writes that Peter, James and John

> crossed over from the flesh to the spirit, having already put off their carnal life. The Spirit brought about a transformation of their sensible energies and stripped away the veils of passion from their intellectual faculty. Having been cleansed by the Spirit in their psychic and bodily senses, they were taught the spiritual principles of the mysteries that had been exhibited to them.[10]

Here we find the synergistic property at work: the disciples "having already put off their carnal life," and "the Spirit brought about a transformation." This event exemplifies how the Spirit enhances the believer's efforts.

By no means does this example suggest that such an experience will happen to everyone. Though it should be mentioned that in *The Acquisition of the Holy Spirit: A Conversation of St. Seraphim of Sarov and N. A. Motovilov*, a similar incident occurs. Motovilov sees St. Seraphim's face radiating like the sun, only to discover moments later that he too is transfigured.[11]

Can the layperson expect to become truly pure in heart, pure in the sense that we can experience that which Thomas Merton and St. Gregory of Nyssa explained? Probably not. But again, the ability to see God is not something one either has or does not have. It is best described (though never measured) as occurring in degrees. And one may even say it can be somewhat fleeting. In the case of Motovilov, we see a man whose eyes are opened; yet there is no mention of this type of experience occurring again. We can assume it probably did not. Yet the reason for desiring to see God in such a way should not be for having some "spiritual" experience. To be in search for experiences is to be open for *prelest* or deception.

Our desire should be to know God and to become what He has created us to be. In achieving this state, we may expect to have our "inner eyes" opened, if only for short periods, to see creation as it really is. Furthermore, we may discover the kingdom of God within us (Luke 17:21), if we see through eyes not blinded by guile and sin.

For some, the idea of seeing God, the transformation of our inner eye may seem like pie-in-the-sky mysticism that has little to do with the Church and her mission. Yet the ability by God's grace to see the world as well as our brothers, sisters, and neighbors in the way that God intended us to see them should have a radical effect on the way we live our everyday lives. In fact, it could be said that such a transformation is at the heart of the Church's life and mission. St. Seraphim of Sarov once said, "Acquire a peaceful spirit and thousands around you will be saved." As we enter into the work of our salvation —the struggle with the passions, the participation in Church life, the communion of the saints, the cleansing of our hearts— we grow closer to the person that God created us to be. The new way of seeing, the saving of "thousands around you," is merely what can occur as we grow in the likeness of God.

By studying the teachings of the Church and of her saints, we learn how to begin this journey, a journey that is one of struggle and difficulty, and one that paradoxically begins in and leads to the Kingdom of God.

Essence and Energies

When the Holy Fathers speak of seeing or knowing God, they differentiate between God's *essence* and His *energies*. While many of the Fathers make this distinction, St. Gregory Palamas is the most widely known for his expositions on this subject. His explanation goes far beyond our present scope. It is important, however, to have an understanding of how the two differ. In doing so, we gain a clearer understanding of the seemingly contradictory references found in Scripture that we have discussed.

Metropolitan Kallistos Ware explains: "God's essence remains unapproachable, but His energies come down to us."[12] The essence of God is that which remains transcendent, thus unknowable and inapproachable. Hence we find statements both in the Old and New Testaments that speak of the inability to see God (Ex 33:20 and Jn 1:18); yet through His energies, He communicates to us. The energies of God are the "qualities," for lack of a better word, or that which we can know about Him. Through His activities we are able to know Him. Thus we see God, not in His transcendent holiness, but in His manifestations or self-revelations.

We know that God is love, and we experience His love in various ways. By seeing God's creation, we may ascertain that He is wise and a lover of beauty. In such ways God manifests Himself to us so that we may know Him and worship Him. Such are the energies of God. They are not separate from Him anymore than what we say and do is separate from us. Again, Ware writes, "The energies are truly God *himself*—yet not God as he communicates himself in outgoing love."[13] In the same way, a work of art tells us something about the artist, but it does not allow us to know the inner workings of the artist, the true self.

The more we purify our hearts, the more we see what *is*, not the false reality that we see through a veil of selfishness, greed, and lust. We begin seeing God at work in His creation, in His people, and in His Church. In doing so, we *see* God in the present! Or perhaps more accurately, we become aware that He is present and fills all things.

This conscious awareness is the beginning of seeing the world and each other, not as we have been taught or socialized to see, but as God has intended us to see. By applying the words of Scripture and the teaching of the Holy Fathers, we can gain a clearer vision of our life and the world around us.

First, we will look at what God created us to be, what it means to be created in the image and likeness of God. This understanding leads us to see ourselves and others in a different light. Also, we must gain a proper view of God's creation. Much is being said about our environment. Many of the comments are quite negative, even hostile, toward the Christian faith. As we shall see, these arguments stem from a complete misunderstanding of the true, Christian teachings on nature and our responsibility toward it. (This misunderstanding is found also in Christian circles who have little knowledge of the teachings of the Fathers and the early Church.)

Finally, we will explore what such a transformed vision entails and what are the subsequent responsibilities inherent for those who embark on this path.

2

The Human Person as Image and Likeness

A cursory examination of the Orthodox teaching on the human person is important to our understanding of who we are and who our neighbor is. Without this knowledge we are apt to float in the modern sea of uncertainty, believing we came from nothing, have no real purpose, and are going nowhere. It is no wonder that in our times such an emphasis is placed on building self-esteem in our young people. Having taken away the belief that we are created in the image and likeness of God, school systems and mental health workers slave at trying to build self-esteem without any solid or true foundation.

We must therefore have the proper understanding of the human person in order to perceive accurately ourselves and others. The pure in heart see beyond the pettiness and sinfulness of humankind, glimpsing in others the divine image, which has been distorted by sin. For those of us who have yet to reach this state of perfection, we must consciously remind ourselves of who we and who others are. If not, it is easy for our hearts to harden, to become cynical and callous. Indeed, Christ warned us that such coldness will overcome most people: "Because of the increase of wickedness, the love of most will grow cold" (Matt 24:12 NIV). Perhaps this "increase in wickedness" causes us to forget that the people who are becoming increasingly rude, insensitive, selfish, and violent are still created in God's image. They still have, no matter how distorted, the stamp of the Divine Creator. We must not forget this truth. If we do, our hearts will harden and compassion will cease. Our society as a whole has forgotten, or in most cases, has never known what the early Church believed about the human person. Such ignorance has led to the slaughter of millions of unborn babies as well as an ethical ambiguity regarding "assisted suicides" and hosts of other legal crimes. Moreover, many believe little difference exists between humans and animals, in the area of rights. Some activists are against the killing of animals for the making of fur coats, but advocate the woman's right to destroy a human life, if having a child inhibits her lifestyle in some way.

First, the account of creation found in Genesis tells us that we are created in the image of God: "God created man in his own image, in the image of God he created him; male and female he created them" (Gen 1:27). The preceding verse tells us that God had decreed that man be created in His image and likeness.

But what does it mean to be created in the image and likeness of God? Is there a difference between image and likeness? If so, what does each entail? Some of the Holy Fathers made no distinction between the two terms; the majority, however, did. It seems that the conjunction *and* denotes a difference. We don't say, for example, that the sky is blue *and* blue. If no distinction exists, then the statement "image and likeness" is redundant. Thus we will focus on the teachings of the Fathers who saw the distinction. Protopresbyter Michael Pomazansky explains quite succinctly:

> [The Holy Fathers] see the image of God in the very *nature* of the soul, and the likeness in the moral *perfecting* of man in virtue and sanctity, in the acquirement of the gifts of the Holy Spirit. Consequently, we receive the image of God from God together with existence, but the likeness we must acquire ourselves, having received the possibility of doing this from God.[1]

In other words, the image of God is a part of being human. *Every* person is created in God's image. This "stamp" of the Divine cannot be taken away. We achieve the likeness of God, however, as we grow in our Christian lives, through repentance, asceticism, and participation in the life of the Church.

Ware explains the terms in much the same way. According to Ware, the Greek Fathers who drew a line between image and likeness agreed that the former is static and the latter is dynamic. Ware writes that the image "denotes man's *potentiality* for life in God, the likeness his *realization* of that potentiality. The image is that which man possesses from the beginning, and which enables him to set out in the first place upon the spiritual Way; the likeness is that which he hopes to attain at his journey's end."[2]

The *image* therefore is shared by all of humanity, thus making human nature "very good" (Gen 1:31). Although sin entered the world through Adam, bringing death and distortion, it is impossible that we, no matter how perverse or corrupted we become, will lose the image. Regarding the results of the Fall, Ware writes, "The divine image in man was obscured but not obliterated."[3] Even many Christians fail to understand this important truth. The concept of original guilt that has strayed into a teaching believed by a significant body of Western Christianity is that we are depraved worms, in whom no good could exist. This belief implies that through the Fall, God's image was distorted to the degree of being negligible. Salvation through "amazing grace" was able to save "a wretch like me." The more Orthodox traditional and especially eastern understanding is, however, quite different. Christ came to restore each person to his or her original "goodness."

The Person as Image

If the image of God is our potentiality for life in God, how and by what means is the image manifested? What is the human person in relation to the rest of creation? Fr. Michael Pomazansky describes human beings as being the crown of creation: "In the ladder of the earthly creation, man is placed on the highest rung, and in relationship to all earthly beings he occupies the reigning positions."[4] Pomazansky states that we surpass all other creatures, because we are created with a soul. Each person "is a living, organic union of the earthly and the heavenly, the material and the spiritual," having been formed from the earthly elements and having received God's breath of life (Gen 2:7).[5]

Much of the West has viewed Adam as having been created perfect in actuality and not potentiality. The Eastern view is different. Adam was perfect in that he had the potential for growing in the likeness of God: "Endowed with the image from the start, he was called to acquire likeness by his own efforts (assisted of course by the grace of God)."[6] Adam failed to fulfill his potential, and sin entered the world. But, as we have seen, this failure did not destroy the image still within him.

This image is seen in the soul itself. "Man bears the image of God in the higher qualities of the soul, especially in the soul's immortality, in its freedom of will, reason, and in its capability for pure love without thought of gain."[7] Thus God is immortal; so is the soul. God is free; so too are we in a more limited sense. God is wise; so He has given us reason, which allows us to understand aspects of the physical and spiritual life. God is love; so too does our soul long to love others.

It is no exaggeration to say that each person "is a 'living theology,' and because he is God's icon, he can find God by looking within his own heart, by returning within himself."[8] No other creature has this capacity. As we shall see later, the early Fathers place much emphasis on this ability to see God within.

Sin and Its Effects on the Image

We are, according to the Church, so good and are held in such an exalted position, why, one might ask, do we see such ugliness and evil manifesting itself in ourselves and others around us? Is not such an optimistic view naive at best or, worse, just plain false? We must remind ourselves that what we are is not tantamount to what we were created to be. Our hope is that we will increasingly become what God intended us to be. Like a snake shedding the old skin we must cast off our sins so that we may grow more into His likeness, our original purpose, our true self.

It is sin that tarnishes the image of God within us. Sin blinds us to who we are and keeps us from penetrating the goodness of creation. Moreover, sin distorts us so that only the pure in heart can see past the layers of filth and falsity that hides the image of God within us. St. Gregory of Nyssa compares this process with that of cleaning iron:

> If freed from rust by a whetstone, that which
> a moment ago was black will shine and glisten
> brightly in the sun. So it is also with the inner
> man, which the Lord calls the heart. When he
> has scraped off the rustlike dirt which dark

decay has caused to appear on his form, he will once more recover the likeness of the archetype [God] and be good.[9]

Recovering then that image is to move closer to the likeness of God; it is to gain the vision of the pure in heart.

We could say therefore without hesitation that we were created to be like God in purity and in love. This state is what is *natural* for us, not the sinful and selfish individuals we have become. Accordingly, it is incorrect for a person to say, "It's natural to sin. Everyone does." While everyone may sin, it is certainly not "natural." In fact, sin is the most *unnatural* aspect of human life. We were not created to sin, but to live a life of holiness and purity. Put another way, to be more godlike is to be more human and to be more human is to be more godlike.

All this talk of the goodness of the human person (in its natural state) begs a question: What exactly is good? the soul? or the body? The answer is "yes" to both. A number of writers have regarded the body as evil and the soul is seen as good. In doing so, we create an unnatural dichotomy between the two. Some borrow from the

Platonists and view the body as a prison for the soul. This doctrine, with its many variations, is foreign to Eastern Christian concepts of the person.

The understanding of the Orthodox Church is that the two—the soul and body—are companions, or at least should be. When the body commits unnatural acts, it places itself at odds with the soul. Pomazansky writes:

> The body must serve as the companion, organ, and even fellow laborer of the soul. It depends on the soul itself whether to lower itself to such an extent that it becomes the slave of the body, or, being guided by an enlightened spirit, to make the body its obedient executor and fellow-laborer. Depending on the soul, the body can be a vessel of sinful impurity and foulness, or it can become the temple of God, participating with the soul in the glorification of God.[10]

The harmonious action of the soul and body in obedience to God is to become fully human. We must remember that even at death the two are not separated forever: "The time will come when the bodies of men will arise in a renewed form and will again be united forever with their souls, in order to receive a part in eternal blessedness or torment, corresponding to the good or evil deeds performed by men with the participation of the body in the course of earthly life."[11] Until that time, however, we will continue to struggle, attempting to purify ourselves by not allowing our passions to rule us.

At the root of Adam's sin, and all sin, is a desire to be autonomous from God. Such a desire grows from our pride: a false belief in our own self-sufficiency. Adam's sin, as well as our own, is to reject communion with God in favor of temporal pleasure. When we reject God's providence and communion, we leave an emptiness in our hearts that is meant to be filled with God's love. This emptiness, this loss of love and relationship typically leaves us feeling lonely and anxious. The result is that human nature becomes fragmented, acting and behaving in ways that are contrary to our calling, contrary to our nature. "The natural needs of the individual being, such as nourishment, self-perpetuation and self-preservation, become an end in themselves: they dominate man, and end up as 'passions,' causes of anguish and the utmost pain, and ultimately the cause of death."[12]

43

The eastern belief differs from the Western view of original sin. Many Christians view sin as some physical taint of guilt that is inherited, transmitted through sexual intercourse. The Eastern view is less juridical and biological. Ware explains,

> The doctrine of original sin means rather that we are born into an environment where it is easy to do evil and hard to do good; easy to hurt others, and hard to heal their wounds; easy to arouse man's suspicions, and hard to win their trust. It means that we are each of us conditioned by the solidarity of the human race in its accumulated wrong-doing and wrong-thinking, and hence wrong-being.[13]

We are not inherently evil, for we are created in the image of God. All creation, as we have seen, is good (Gen 1:36). Yet because sin entered the world, it is difficult to do what is right, to be fully human.

Sin can be seen then as doing that which is contrary to our nature. Christos Yannaras describes sin as "an active refusal on man's part to be what he truly is: the image and 'glory,' or manifestation, of God."[14] To sin or not to sin is a choice between life and death, between the natural and unnatural. Not only are we created in God's image and likeness, but we are also created for communion with God. Each time we sin we refuse this communion, choosing our own individual will over the will of God.

It should be no surprise then that a society that has largely forgotten or never knew why they were created would be so consumed with self-esteem issues, so lost in a sea of therapy, self-help books, and "spiritual experiences." By refusing to live in the way we were created to live, we find an existential void in our lives, a restless, constant search for some new entertainment that will divert our attention away from the emptiness in our souls. And to say one is Christian and therefore exempt from such social pathologies is a crucial mistake. To be a "Christian" in our pluralistic, sectarian-minded society means little. The term is used so loosely that the meaning is all but lost. We can believe and practice a variety of lifestyles and still consider ourselves "Christian." The fact is, however, that statistics show a negligible difference in numbers of divorces and reported abortions between "Christians" and non-Christians.[15]

The importance therefore of understanding the early Christian teachings on the human person is essential. This is especially true since our culture has so many mixed and false notions about human nature. Much of Western Christianity views the human person as evil, a worm and a wretch, believing that the Fall completely obliterated the image and likeness of God. Others have gone to the other extreme and have exalted humanity to a near-deity, seeing little or no distinction between the person and the Divine. For them sin is merely a weakness or a dysfunction that the right amount of treatment (therapy, medication, or social programs) can cure. (If it is not cured, it can be "worked out" in the next life.) Further, some see sin as an individual expression, a right not to be denied.

For many, however, such teachings fly in the face of the reality they experience. Having school children "visualize" themselves as near-perfect people moving toward perfection, without any real struggle or asceticism, will not raise that ever-elusive god we call self-esteem. Even young people, perhaps better than some adults, see through such an illusion. They may not verbalize or even be able to articulate it, but something hollow and untrue reverberates through their being when they are repeatedly told, almost in mantra form, they are "special," that they are "good." It is not, of course, that such claims are wrong; it is that they lack foundation.

Self-esteem should be based on the knowledge and realization that we are created in the image and likeness of God. Self-esteem without this recognition is pride. When the Fathers speak of the sin of self-esteem it is this that they had in mind. It is the sin of Adam and Eve: the attempt to become god without God; to be "good" without reference to the source of goodness. Knowing that we are created in the image of God and that we are loved by Him and have the potential not only for communion with Him but also, by His grace and our efforts, the opportunity to grow into His likeness, is a cause for "self-esteem" in the Christian sense. In this way we are aware of our goodness as well as our short-comings. Moreover, the Church gives us the "prescription," the means to come to grips with our weaknesses and sins and to overcome them in hope and love. In doing so, as we shall see, we grow in the likeness of God.

The Person as Likeness

What does it mean to be created in the likeness of God? As noted earlier, *likeness* refers to our potentiality. Georgios I. Mantzaridis writes, "The word 'likeness,' as used in the Septuagint, expresses something dynamic and not yet realized, whereas the word 'image' signifies a realized state, which in the present context constitutes the starting point for the attainment of the 'likeness.'[16] Such a state, or way of being, is the goal of existence.

Another term that is often used to describe "likeness" is *deification* or *theosis*. Here, by God's grace and the person's efforts, one becomes united with God, while remaining distinct from God. Ware explains that the human person "does not become God *by nature*, but is merely a 'created god,' a god *by grace* or *by status*."[17] In other words, although we are united with "the divine, man still remains man; he is not swallowed up or annihilated, but between him and God there continues always to exist an 'I-Thou' relationship of person to person."[18] Further, this participation in the Divine is a participation in God's *energies*, not His *essence*. Thus we have the potential of becoming like God and completely united with God, but not becoming God Himself. The distinction is important. The Orthodox Church does not teach pantheism, as we shall see more clearly later. While a bridge is erected between Creator and creation, the essence of both God and the person remains unchanged.

We find the scriptural basis for this teaching in several places. For example, in the priestly prayer of Christ, Jesus prays that all believers "may be one, Father, just as you are in me and I am in you. May they also be in us so that the world may believe that you have sent me" (Jn 17:21 NIV). Not only are we one with God, but also one with each other. Deification is mentioned in St. Peter's second epistle: "His divine power has granted to us all things that pertain to life and godliness, through the knowledge of him who called us to his own glory and excellence, by which he has granted to us his precious and very great promises, that

49

through these you may escape from the corruption that is in the world because of passion, and become partakers to the divine nature" (II Pet 1:3-4).

Ware gives six points regarding deification, which help clarify the Church's teaching: First, he reiterates what was stated earlier, that is, deification is not "reserved for a few select initiates, but something intended for all alike." While the process begins here and now, it is not completed or fully realized until the Last Day, at the fulfillment of the Kingdom of God.

Second, being deified does not mean we cease to be conscious of sin. "On the contrary deification always presupposes a continued act of repentance." While Orthodox theology emphasizes "a theology of glory and of transfiguration," it is also "a theology of penitence."

Third, we must realize that the *means* to deification are simple: "go to church, receive the sacraments regularly, pray to God 'in spirit and in truth,' read the Gospels, and follow the commandments."

Fourth, "deification is not a solitary but a 'social' process." To follow the commandments of God we must love others. We are not "saved" alone. Loving our neighbor is essential to the Christian life. For as the Trinity dwell together as one, in love and communion, so must we live and love in communion with others.

Fifth, "love of God and of other men must be practical." St. John Maximovitch "taught that, for all the 'mysticism' of our Orthodox Church that is found in the Lives of Saints and the writings of the Holy Fathers, the truly Orthodox person always has both feet firmly on the ground, facing whatever situation is right in front of him."[19] As Ware points out, some great saints' lives are more "mystical" than others. One thinks of St. Seraphim of Sarov, St. Symeon the New Theologian, or the Hesychasts praying in silence; "but we must also think of Saint Basil caring for the sick in the hospital at Caesarea, of Saint John the Almsgiver helping the poor at Alexandria, of Saint Sergius in his filthy clothing, working as a peasant in the kitchen garden to provide the guests of the monastery with food. These are not two different ways, but one."

Sixth, "deification presupposes life in the Church, life in the sacraments."[20] Through the Church we can be transformed into the divine likeness. It is not enough to belong to the Church. We must instead participate deeply in her life: by partaking regularly of the sacraments; of praying together as a body; by fasting and practicing the acts of asceticism prescribed by Her; by giving alms to the poor and practicing acts of love. Without the life in the Church, deification is impossible. These acts make up the whole. "It is above all through Communion that the Christian is made one with and in Christ, 'christified,' 'ingodded' or 'deified'; it is above all through Communion that he receives the first fruits of eternity."[21]

Thus, the Church views the human person as good. Though tainted by sin, we, by God's grace and our efforts, have the potential to grow in His likeness. Our lives as well as our perception of the world is transformed. We begin seeing beyond the surface, seeing the image and the potential likeness of God in everyone. We see creation as filled with His presence.

Again, it bears repeating, such a state comes slowly, not without great effort and struggle. Yet as we patiently move in this direction we must remind ourselves of these truths that often contradict what we see and what we have been taught. We must bear in mind that God's creation is good; each part of it is a manifestation of God's love; and each person is not only loved by God, but created in His image with the *potential* of growing in union and communion with Him, that is, to become deified.

3

The Mystical Vision: Seeing Beyond the Veil

When our vision is transformed we experience the world in a different way. When we receive glimpses beyond the veil, we are seeing as if through the eyes of the saints. We foretaste what was beheld by those who have struggled and fought the good fight to purify their hearts. For the rest of us who are still struggling, God grants us moments when we *see* with greater clarity the nature of reality, the true essence of Creation. As William Blake once wrote, "We ever must believe a lie/ When we see with not thro' the eye."

We have seen how the Holy Fathers regard the Transfiguration of our Lord as an example of seeing the true nature of Christ. They taught that the real

55

transfiguration occurred in the eyes of the disciples. When our eyes are opened, when we see through and not with them, the world is transformed. We begin seeing ourselves, others, and nature as we are supposed to see them: icons of the transcendent God. We were not created to experience life as an endless series of days, filled with monotony and boredom. Through the Incarnation, Christ has restored meaning and beauty to the fallen world. And while we may not always experience life as meaningful or beautiful, we must remind ourselves to believe that there is more to our lives than what meets the eye; there is more to our world than what we see when our hearts are impure and divided.

God's creation, both nature and humankind, are icons of the transcendent God. Through sin these icons may lose their luster, but they are icons nonetheless. Our priestly calling is not only to recognize this truth but to fulfill it: to be transformed and to transform the world around us.

In the Orthodox services, the opening prayers include an invocation to the Holy Spirit:

> O Heavenly King, the Comforter, Spirit of Truth,
>
> Who are present everywhere and fillest all things...

God is everywhere and fills all His creation. All of creation makes known the Creator. What is sad about modern life is that much of nature is being destroyed, leaving fewer and fewer "signposts" that point to our Creator. Certainly one of the most obvious signs of how far our culture has strayed from God can be found in our cities: huge, often ugly monuments that speak only of our alienation from God and from ourselves. Moreover, the human person, the greatest icon of God, through sin and self-will, has become more and more distorted as society continually drifts further from God. With such perversion of creation and with the elimination of most religious signs or symbols in public places, we easily forget God. When asked how Holy Russia could have ever fallen into the barbarism of the Bolsheviks, Alexander Solzhenitsyn replied, "They forgot God."

Still, Christ's promise for the pure in heart was not time-limited. While it may be more difficult today, living in what many call "the post-Christian world," it is not impossible. For Christ's words are eternal. St. Gregory of Nyssa writes, "He does not tell those He has not provided with wings to become birds, nor does He bid creatures He has destined to sojourn on land to live in the water. The law is adapted to the capacities of those that receive it in everything else, and nothing is enforced that is beyond nature."[1]

It is important to understand what Scripture and the Holy Fathers teach concerning these ideas. In today's world it would be too easy to mistake these teachings as similar to many New Age notions and beliefs, including pantheism. Such ideas are in contrast to the teachings of the Church. By looking at nature, ourselves, and others, we should see an icon of the transcendent God.

Nature

Probably no religion has taken more criticism from environmental groups than has Christianity. Many see the

Christian faith as one that promotes "subduing the earth," based on a misinterpretation of Genesis 1:28-30. Indeed, throughout history Christians themselves have invited such criticism by ignoring their responsibility to creation, using it, abusing it, and manipulating it so to create greater financial profit.

Let us look closely at the words from this misinterpreted text:

> And God blessed [Adam and Eve], and God said to them, "Be fruitful and multiply, and fill the earth and subdue it; and have dominion over the fish of the sea and over the birds of the air and over every living thing that moves on the earth." And God said, "Behold, I have given you every plant yielding seed which is upon the face of all the earth, and every tree with seed in its fruit; you shall have them for food. And to every beast of the earth, and to every bird of the air, and to everything that creeps on the earth, everything that has the breath of life, I have given every green plant for food." And it was so. (Gen. 1:28-30)

From this passage we see that it makes more sense to interpret this charge as a call for stewardship. God gave man the ultimate responsibility of tending the earth. The passage should not be seen as a license for us to exploit the earth for our own gain. Creation is a gift. Why would God would give us a gift, a gift which He describes as being "very good," just so that we could destroy it? We are to be stewards of the land, not manipulators and exploiters.

How much more does this seem true if we view nature as an icon of its Creator? St. Paul declares that no one can escape God's wrath, because His creation speaks forth of His glory and existence to all: "Ever since the creation of the world his invisible nature, namely, his eternal power and deity, has been clearly perceived in the things that have been made. So they are without excuse" (Romans 1:20). St. Gregory of Nyssa echoes this idea:

> For it is possible to see Him who has *made all things in wisdom* by way of inference through the wisdom that appears in the universe. It is the same as with human works of art where, in a way, the mind can perceive the maker of the product that is before it, because he has left on his work the stamp of his art.... Thus also, when we look at the order of creation, we form in our mind an image not of the

essence, but of the wisdom of Him who made all things wisely.[2]

St. Maximus the Confessor states, "We do not know God in his essence. We know him rather from the grandeur of His creation and from his providential care for all creatures. For by the means, as if using a mirror, we may attain insight into his infinite goodness, wisdom and power."[3] We can know the attributes or the energies of God through His creation.

We find a passage in the Wisdom of Solomon that speaks of God revealing Himself through His creation. Much like what the Apostle Paul teaches in the first chapter of Romans, the writer declares that God can be known through creation (or at least His existence can be confirmed) but people fail to understand that God is the Creator. Instead, the foolish keep searching, failing to understand or misunderstanding the signs given to them.

> For all men who were ignorant of God were foolish by nature; and they were unable from the good things that are seen to know him who exists, nor did they recognize the craftsman while paying heed to his works; but they supposed that either fire or wind or swift

air, or the circle of the stars, or turbulent water, or the luminaries of heaven were the gods that ruled the world. If through delight in the beauty of these things men assumed them to be gods, let them know how much better than these is their Lord, for the author of beauty created them. And if men were amazed at their power and working let them perceive from them how much more powerful is he who formed them. For from the greatness and beauty of created things comes a corresponding perception of their Creator. (Wisdom of Solomon 13:1-5)

Therefore, while nature is an icon of God the revelation it gives forth is incomplete. We may know of God's majesty, wisdom, and beauty through nature, but because of our sinfulness, because of our inclination to follow the self and not God, the picture is distorted. This explains why so many who love the environment do not "recognize the craftsman while paying heed to the works." As the poet Elizabeth Barrett Browning wrote:

> Earth's crammed with heaven,
> And every common bush afire with God;
> But only he who sees, takes off his shoes,
> The rest sit round it and pluck blackberries,
> And daub their natural faces unaware

More and more from the first similitude.

With a pure heart, however, our vision becomes clearer. We do not rely solely on our own interpretation of what we see; instead, through the sacraments and through our life in the Church, we are given a foundation on which to build, a framework through which to view nature. With this understanding and with the grace that is found through prayer and the sacraments we can perceive "from the greatness and beauty of created things comes a corresponding perception of their Creator." One should not confuse this teaching with the pantheistic beliefs of other religions. Unlike other religions Christianity teaches that God is uncreated; therefore He is wholly Other, yet still "fills all things." Ware explains, "As Christians we offer not pantheism but 'panentheism.' God is *in* all things yet also *beyond and above* all things. In the words of St. Gregory of Palamas, 'He is everywhere and nowhere, he is everything and nothing.'[4] This distinction is important for us to remember. While God manifests Himself in Creation, He is *not* nature itself. Nature is the work of His hands. While He "fills all things" He is not all things. "God is above and outside His creation, yet He also exists within it."[5]

Many view the land as something that does little more than yield a profit. For them nature is not to be tended and given back to God, but exploited and manipulated, producing disastrous results. Yet this is not surprising. The Apostle Paul wrote: "To the pure all things are pure, but to the corrupt and unbelieving nothing is pure" (Titus 1:15). What is a shame is that throughout history many have stripped and destroyed the land in the name of Christ. But for those who are pure in heart, nature glorifies God and makes manifest His attributes. For this reason, Fr. Zosima, the famous elder of Dostoevsky's *The Brothers Karamazov*, states:

> Love all God's creation, the whole and every grain of sand in it. Love every leaf, every ray of God's light. Love the animals, love the plants, love everything. If you love everything, you will perceive the divine mystery in things. Once you perceive it, you will begin to comprehend it better every day. And you will come at last to love the whole world with an all-embracing love.[6]

In short, all creation should be revered, for it is a reflection, an icon of the Creator. As each work of art carries with it a part of the artist, the same is true for all creation, both animate and inanimate. The psalmists sings:

The heavens are telling the glory of God;
and the firmament proclaims his handiwork.

Day to day pours forth speech,
and night to night declares knowledge.

There is no speech, nor are there words;
their voice is not heard;

yet their voice goes out through all the earth,
and their words to the end of the world. (Ps. 19:1-4)

We, as Christians, need to recognize the importance of creation and not fall into a false dualism, pitting the spiritual against the material world, as if they are completely separate. Ware writes, "The Christian is the one who, wherever he looks, sees God everywhere and rejoices in him. Not without reason did the early Christians attribute to Christ this saying: "Lift the stone and you will find me; cut the wood in two and there I am."[7] Similarly St. Basil the Great states, "I want creation to penetrate you with so much admiration that everywhere, wherever you may be, the least plant may bring to you the remembrance of the Creator."

Much of the criticism of Christianity that comes from environmentalists is unjust. While no doubt the fall resulted in an under-appreciation, if not abuse, of the natural world, it is wrong to conclude that Christian teaching instructs us to be indifferent or, worse, antagonistic toward creation. In fact, the late Patriarch Dimitrios of Constantinople declared that September 1, the beginning of the ecclesiastical year, be established as a special feast day, the Protection of the Environment. "Orthodox Perspective on Creation" was the theme of an Inter-Orthodox Consultation held in Sofia. Some of the main points that were confirmed include:

> The value of creation lies in its intrinsic goodness, but also in the fact that God appointed it "to be the home of living beings." It is "the context for God's Incarnation and mankind's deification, and as such, the beginning of the actualization of the Kingdom of God."

> The fall of humanity led to the disintegration of the creation. Caused by sinful exercises of

human freedom, the fall resulted in a two-fold alienation: "On the one hand, [humanity] was estranged from the Creator, since Adam and Eve tended to hide themselves away from the sight of God (cf. Gen. 3:8);...on the other hand, humanity lost its capacity to enter into a proper relation with nature and with the body of creation."

Environmental issues threaten the life itself on this planet. The gifts of science and technology are being misused by human beings to the extent of abusing nature and turning earth into a hell for the generations to come.

Inasmuch as humanity was created in the likeness of God, it was entrusted with the task of perfecting not only human nature, but also the created nature which forms its natural habitants.

Humanity can no longer ignore its responsibility to protect and preserve creation; humanity, must learn to treat the creation as a sacred offering to God, an obligation, a vehicle of grace, an incarnation of our most noble aspirations and prayers....We are called to offer the whole of God's creation back to Him as a sacrament and as an offering cleansed, purified, restored for His sanctification of it.[8]

While some may argue that such responses are "too little too late," we need to remember that these instructions are not a recent response to a modern crisis; they are, instead, the teachings of the Holy Fathers, a part of the patristic world view that has, in most areas, been lost.

Our response to criticism over environmental issues must be two-fold: First, despite the exalted teachings we have discussed, we must recognize and repent for living in a way that has contributed to the defacing of the earth. We must share in the blame; for we have failed to learn, much less practice, the patristic ideal. As Brother Arden writes, "And it is all the more important to understand this patristic cosmology because, in ignorance of it, many recent ecologists have taken its distortions—pseudo-Christian rationalism, the Protestant work ethic, tyrannical industrialism, and so on—as the last word on Christian ecology."[9] Second, we must introduce these ancient teachings of the Fathers into our ecological discussions. Christianity has taken too much criticism, most of it undeserved, for us not to offer not only a defense, but a proper way of understanding the environment and our role within it.

We must realize that our spiritual health, our very calling as human beings, is to be priests, to be mediators between God and His creation: "The work of a priest is to offer, to sacrifice. The priest is the mediator who takes what is below him—the material world—and offers it, and through it, offers himself to God who is above all."[10] An example of using a part of creation (wine and bread) and offering it to God can be found in the Divine Liturgy: "We offer you what is your own from your own on behalf of all and for all." We must offer creation to God and be stewards of the gift He has given us. Moreover, we must not forget that creation is the work of God and it is good. By contemplating nature we discover God. For "contemplation of God in his creation is an essential part of our preparation for our union with God."[11] It is therefore a contradiction to believe that one can be spiritually sound and environmentally indifferent. The key for us is to regain the patristic view that has been handed down, yet often ignored, and to be transformed by it while transforming the world around us.

The Self

The Church views the human person as good, a reflection of the Divine. We are created in His image and have the potential to achieve, in varying degrees, His likeness. The Holy Fathers teach that, not only can we know God through nature, but we can also know Him through ourselves. If God reveals Himself in all created things, the clearest example of such a revelation can be found in the very image of God, that is, the human person.

For example, St. Cyprian of Carthage once wrote, "That you may acquaint yourself with God, first become acquainted with yourself."[12] St. Isaac the Syrian states, "To him who knows himself, knowledge of all things is given. For knowing oneself is the fulfillment of the knowledge of all things." He also writes. "Strive to enter the treasury within you and you will see the heavenly treasury; for the two are one and the same. By entering one, you will see both. The ladder to that kingdom is within you, hidden in your soul."[13] St. Anthony of Egypt teaches, "Know yourselves.... He who knows himself, knows God."[14]

For some these sayings may seem presumptuous, even audacious. But the early saints took seriously the idea of the image of God in each person. We are icons of God. It is therefore no surprise that it is within each person that the image of God can be found. As our hearts are purified the image in ourselves, as well as others, becomes clearer. What these saints teach is the same truth that Christ told the Pharisees: "The kingdom of God is with you" (Luke 17:20).

Unfortunately sin has blinded us (or at least impaired our vision), making such perception more difficult. For those whose hearts are not cleansed, looking within oneself may reveal only darkness and deceit. To behold clearly the image of God within ourselves, purity of heart is essential. Ware writes, "Made in God's image, man is the mirror of the divine. He knows God by knowing himself: entering within himself, he sees God reflected in the purity of his own heart."[15] St. Isaac the Syrian writes, "If you are pure, heaven is within you; within yourself you will see the angels and the Lord of angels."[16] St. Maximus the Confessor teaches that God "is hidden in the hearts of those who believe in Him. They shall see Him when they have purified themselves through love and self-control; and the greater the purity, the more they shall see." Similarly, St. Gregory of Nyssa states that "if a man's heart has been purified from every creature and all unruly affections, he will see the image of the Divine Nature in his own beauty."[17] Again, we find that purity of heart and the subsequent ability to see God is not an either/or proposition; it is instead a matter of degrees, a process which, by our efforts and God's grace, will allow us to see more clearly as we grow in His likeness.

Others

It would be a grave mistake to believe that to discover God we must look solely within. He also reveals

Himself in nature. Moreover, introspection alone can lead to a rather narcissistic relationship to God, ego-centered instead of Theo-centered. Consequently, if God is in each one of us, He can be seen in those with whom we have contact. The image of God can be seen in everyone, even those outside the Church.

We should look for the divine image in everyone we meet, honoring the God who resides in each believer. Fr. Thomas Hopko gives us a good example of seeing the divine in others. He writes,

> The holy fathers not only fed those who came to them, even on fasting days, but they ate with them as well. Some of the greatest ascetics would even eat and drink more than those whom they were feeding so that their guests would not feel badly, and so that they themselves would not appear to men to be fasting.[18]

Hopko goes on to tell us of St. Macarius the Great and St. Sisoes, two monastic saints of the early Church. It was said that people were warned not to visit these saints often. Should they visit them, they should eat and drink as little as possible. "For it was the practice of these holy men to fast at least twice as much in secret as they had eaten with their brothers in public. For every piece of bread taken in company, they denied themselves two pieces in private."[19] They did likewise with the amount of wine consumed. When asked why they did this, they referred to the words of Jesus: "As long as they [the disciples] have the bridegroom with them, they cannot fast. The day will come, when the bridegroom is taken away from them, and then they will fast in that day" (Mark 2:19-20). Hopko explains this connection:

> The saints were convinced that every person who came to them was Christ. They fulfilled literally the teaching that whatever was done for the least of the brethren was done to the Lord Himself (Mt. 25:31-46). They believed every guest was the Bridegroom, and when the Bridegroom is present one cannot fast. But when the Bridegroom is taken away, then the people fast.[20]

With pure hearts these saints were able to see God, not in the mystical light of Mount Tabor, but in the people around them. This example does not teach us that we should be undisciplined in our fasting, but that we should "rejoice in our brothers and sisters at all times. That we should see Christ the Bridegroom in their person and presence."[21]

St. Silouan (Silvanus), a monk of Mount Athos who died in 1938, wrote,

> O brethren, there is nothing better than the love of God when the Lord fires the soul with love for God and our fellow-men.... The man who knows the delight of the love of God—when the soul, warmed by grace, loves both God and her brother—knows in part that "the kingdom of God is within us." Blessed is the soul that loves her brother, for our brother is our life.

The Fathers teach us again and again, concurring with Scripture, that our love for God is interrelated, even dependent upon, our love for our neighbor. Christ said the greatest commandment was to love God with all our heart, soul, mind, and strength. This is the first and greatest commandment. Then He said, "And a second is like it, You shall love your neighbor as yourself" (Matt 22:37-39). Without love for others it is impossible to love God (cf. 1

John 2:9). It is impossible to love others, especially those who wrong us, unless we see beyond the surface, unless we see the image of God within them. As stated earlier, this image may be distorted almost beyond recognition, but the image remains nonetheless. Each person we see and meet is loved by God, and God desires that this person love Him and know Him. Further, He desires the salvation of all people, of all races, creeds, and cultures; of the believer and unbelievers; the criminal and the victim.

The importance of viewing each person as special, created in God's image, cannot be overemphasized. Believer and non-believer alike should be treated with love, respect, and compassion. While it is true that our brothers and sisters in Christ have in them the indwelling of the Holy Spirit and are a part of His body and therefore a part of us, we cannot ignore or treat as irrelevant those outside of the Church. Too often in Christendom we have fallen into placing people in "us or them" categories. With this view the world becomes fragmented and alienating. We categorize and polarize the creation of God: the material versus the spiritual; the secular versus the sacred; the believer versus the unbeliever. Even the "believer" category gets broken down into Protestant versus Orthodox versus Catholic. Within the Protestant tradition itself, this breakdown can be endless, as seen in the myriad of denominations. In short, the holistic view of the world has been lost. No sense of unity or oneness exists.

While certain distinctions are crucial, as in the case of determining heresy from true doctrine, less important ones can be limiting. The loss of a certain "us-ness" has been replaced by a needless dichotomous view of the world. The result is that we have isolated ourselves from the rest of creation as if anyone or anything outside our own tradition is superfluous and of no importance. In the spiritual classic *The Way of the Pilgrim*, the writer quotes the Nicetas Stethatos as saying, "He who attains true prayer and love has no sense of the differences between things: he does not distinguish between the righteous man and the sinner, but loves them all equally and judges no man, as God causes His sun to shine and His rain to fall on the just and unjust."[22] Prayer is central to purifying our heart.

For the pure in heart, these distinctions are blurred. They are able to see past the superficialities and see not only the image of God, but also that person's *potential* to grow in the likeness. In his book *Life and Holiness* Thomas Merton makes only a slight distinction in humanity: those who are a part of the body of Christ and those who have the *potential* to be members of the body of Christ. Thus for those who have yet to attain this vision of others, it is helpful to know, to remind ourselves, that each person has the potential to receive salvation from Jesus Christ. And instead of judging unbelievers we must ask ourselves if we are not perhaps part of the reason they do not believe. Elsewhere Merton writes, "Do not be too quick to condemn the man who no longer believes in God. For it is perhaps your own coldness and avarice and mediocrity and materialism and sensuality and selfishness that has killed his faith."

No greater sin can be found than that of Judas the betrayer. Yet in the book of Acts, when Judas was replaced by Matthias, we hear no words of condemnation heaped on the fallen disciple. Peter said, "Brethren, the scripture had to be fulfilled, which the Holy Spirit spoke beforehand by the mouth of David, concerning Judas who was guide to those who arrested Jesus. For he was numbered among us, and was allotted his share in this ministry" (Acts 1:16-17). Concerning this passage, St. John Chrysostom states, "Mark the philosophical temper of Peter: how he does not mention Judas with scorn.... He relates what had been the case with Judas, that from the present one may gain assurance of the future, and show that this man has already received his due." In other words, our place is not to judge; God's merciful judgment will be rendered, without us adding our own blind accusations.

St. Anastasius of Sinai taught that we should not condemn those who sin in public, for they may repent in private. He reminds us that the thief who was crucified next to Christ was a criminal, while Judas was an apostle; yet the thief entered Paradise while Judas went to perdition. Moreover, we cannot see the future. At some point the person may repent and the image of God, so distorted, will become clearer and clearer, so that the likeness of God shows through.

In the parable of the Good Samaritan (Luke 10:30-35), we find that true love for others transcends who the person is and what the person believes. We are to love all without distinction: that is, we are called to love and do good to everyone, not just our brothers and sisters in Christ. Our love should not be limited to those who believe what we believe, yet we are called to an even deeper relationship with our fellow believers. This may sound like a contradiction, considering all that has been said about making distinctions. The point is that we must love and do good to all, without judging or placing others in categories that are inferior to those of our own faith. "Therefore, as we have opportunity, let us do good to all people, especially those who belong to the family of believers" (Gal 6:10 NIV).

We are one with the body of Christ. We must therefore remember that we are dependent on one another (cf. I. Cor 12:12-27). Through our own unity others outside the Church will see God's love manifested. Christ prayed that all believers "may become perfectly one, so that the world may know that thou hast sent me and hast loved them even as thou hast loved me" (John 17:23). Doing good especially "to the family of believers" does not mean that we can treat unbelievers in a condescending way or that we are somehow better than they are. We are called to be one, and by our love for one another God's love will be displayed to this sick and dying world.

The Holy Spirit resides within each believer. Those with a pure heart see God Himself when they see their brother or sister. St. Anthony the Great writes, "Our life and our death is with our neighbor. If we have gained our brother, we have gained God. But if we scandalize our brother, we have sinned against Christ." More directly, Clement of Alexandria states: "When you see your brother, you see God."[23] Merton writes, "Christ is really present in us, more present than if He were standing before us visible to our bodily eyes. For we have become 'other Christs.'"[24]

While we are called to see our brothers and sisters in Christ as those with whom we are one, we must be careful not to view people as being either "in" or "out." For the truly pure in heart, distinctions are blurred. Fr. Seraphim

Rose writes that the Christian "loves his fellow man because he sees in him one created in the image of God and called to perfection and eternal life in God; such love is not human but divine, seeing in men not mere earthly mortality, but heavenly immortality."[25] Merton writes, "If we believe in the Incarnation of the Son of God, there should be no one on earth in whom we are not prepared to see, in mystery, the presence of Christ."[26]

Let us therefore purify our hearts so that we may see God in nature, in ourselves, and in others. While we still are on the arduous path of purification, we must remind ourselves that God is in us and all around us. When we see nature let us be attentive to the message it speaks forth (Ps 19:1-4). When we reflect on our own hearts, let us remember that the Holy Spirit dwells within us who are members of His body. And when we see our neighbor; when we see those we meet each day, let us love them and honor them, realizing that they have been created in God's image and have the potential, just like ourselves, to grow in His likeness. Let us remember the words of St. Macarius: "There is no other way to be saved, except through our neighbor.... This is purity of heart: when you see the sinful or the sick, to feel compassion for them and to be tenderhearted toward them."[27]

4

The Path to Purity

Before exploring the path to purity, we must understand that our spiritual growth is dependent upon our life in the Church. It is through the Church that the Holy Spirit transforms us into the likeness of God. The Holy Mysteries, or what is known in the West as the Sacraments, provide the believer with a means to union with God. As we look at how we can purify our hearts—becomes single-minded—we must realize that this process is not separate or independent of the Church. The path, we could say, is at the heart of the Church, found in the services and practices throughout the year. In other words, we do not walk the path alone; instead, we walk side-by-side with our fellow believers, emulating those who are strong and encouraging those who are weak.

It goes beyond the scope of this book to go into great detail concerning the ways and practices by which the Church strengthens and purifies us. Three practices, however, are central to a life of holiness and purity. They have been called the three-legged stool that supports the believer: fasting, prayer, and almsgiving. They are acts of love and effective weapons in the spiritual warfare. Without actively practicing these acts of love, we will find it difficult, if not impossible, to achieve purity of heart. Not only are these the *means* to purity; they are the fruit born out of a heart that has union with God as its sole intention.

Fasting, prayer, and almsgiving are acts of asceticism, that is, practices of self-restraint and self-denial. But if we are created "good," why do we need to practice self-denial? While it is true that we are created in the image and likeness of God and that we are not born "depraved" or "guilty," there is a force—sin—that is working contrary to our nature (cf. Rom 7:7-25). It is not our nature that is evil, but sin drives us to act in a way that is opposed to our nature. Thus, through asceticism, we attempt to harness and eventually destroy the lusts and passions of our flesh.

St. Symeon the New Theologian writes, "He who pursues his own will, however slightly, will never be able to observe the precepts of Christ the Savior." By saying "no" to our wants and desires, even the ones that are good, such as eating, we develop the discipline to deny those desires that are evil. If we do not refrain from eating breakfast on Sunday morning to prepare for the Eucharist, we will find it more difficult to refrain from opportunities to gossip or indulge in sexual fantasies.

If we live disciplined lives, we have certain times we pray, fast, and give alms. We do so at the given hours or days, whether we want to or not. If we fast only when we are tired of the "same old food" or need to lose a few pounds, we are likely to fail to keep the longer fasts that are prescribed by the Church. If we pray only when we feel like it, our prayers will be short and sporadic. If we give alms or do acts of charity only when we can fit it into our budget or our busy schedules or, worse yet, when we think the person is deserving of our generosity, we will seldom give. By being disciplined in these efforts we learn the "one thing needful"(Luke 10:42); we discover that we live not by "bread" alone (cf. Matt 4:4; Deut 8:3), but our sustenance, our very being, is dependent on God. We strengthen our souls and learn to live a life in the Spirit, a life not controlled by physical wants and desires.

Fasting

Fasting is practiced by many religions. The origins of Christian fasting can be found in Judaism as well as in the pagan religions. While the New Testament gives no specific rules concerning the particular days or times of the year when fasting occurred, we do know that fasting was practiced both by Christ and the Apostles. We also know that, above all, what is more important than the fast itself is the attitude with which one fasts. Fasting should be done in secret (Matt 6:16-18), because this practice easily leads to hypocrisy (cf. Isa 58). Likewise, fasting should be done in humility.

The Jewish tradition called for fasting on Monday and Thursday. The early Christians gave new meaning to fasting and therefore changed the days to Wednesday and

Friday: "Wednesday because on this day the Jews conspired against Christ, and Friday because it was the day of His crucifixion."[1] The regulations and practices of fasting have varied at different times and places. Most of the rules were established for the monastic life and are seldom practiced in full by the laity during our contemporary times. Still, fasting is not to be under-emphasized as something anachronistic or a feat performed only by saints. It is an essential part of the life of the Church, a means to purity of heart.

The yearly cycle of services and feast days contains many appointed fasts. Perhaps the one most practiced is that of Great Lent, a forty-day period that prepares us for Pascha or Easter, the celebration of the Resurrection. The Advent, or Nativity fast, is also forty days. Other feasts that are preceded by periods of fasting include the fast of the Holy Apostles, ending with the feast of Sts. Peter and Paul; a two-week fast preceding the Dormition of the Mother of God; the day before Theophany; and finally both the Beheading of the Forerunner and the Exaltation of the Cross are strict fast days. Each Wednesday and Friday, except when coinciding with a feast, are days of fasting. Fasting is also practiced on the Lord's Day, Sunday, as a means for preparing to receive Holy Communion. No food or drinks are allowed from midnight until the time we receive the Eucharist. (It should be noted that the Church recognizes our frailty, knowing that some are too sick or weak to fast. In such cases, the priest can make allowances for those who have medical problems that prevent them from fully participating in the fast.)

What do we mean by fasting? While true fasting is the abstention from food, the actual practice is obviously not this strict. Within the tradition of the Church, the practice of fasting has varied. As a general rule the Orthodox Church instructs us that during a fast we should abstain from meat, fish, and dairy products. Before receiving Holy Communion and on feast days that call for a strict fast, food and drinks are prohibited. According to Stanley Harakas, within the Church canons only one set of rules exist; these rules refer to Great Lent, "the most severe of the periodic fasts." The rule is known as "dry eating," "which excludes meat, fish, alcoholic beverages, eggs, milk, cheese, and oil. That leaves bread, water and vegetables."[2] Such strict fasting is usually found only in monasteries. We should make a point, however, to abstain as much as possible and practice the fast in the best way we can, in accordance with our parish priest or spiritual father. The absolute minimum one can do is to abstain from meat. Thus, for the Orthodox, fasting is probably best defined as abstention, except on certain appointed days and prior to Holy Communion.

But it is possible to practice the fasts strictly and still fall into error. Fasting is more than just a denial of certain foods or drinks. Our fasting must include abstinence from sin. A hymn sung on the first Monday of Great Lent states that a "true fast is the estrangement from evil, temperance of tongue, abstinence from anger, separation from desires, slander, falsehood, perjury. Privation of these is true fasting." Leo the Great warns: "We withhold delicacies from our bodies in vain unless our hearts refrain from iniquity and the tongue is restrained from speaking evil."

Any ascetic act, especially fasting, forces us to struggle against hypocrisy. When we view fasting as an end and not a means to holiness we fall into the sin of the Pharisees. Instead of making us more humble, realizing our dependence on God, we take pride in our ascetic feat and, worse yet, look down on those who fail to understand or practice what we do. If our fasting causes us to become proud or irritable, then we are missing the true meaning of the fast. In Isaiah we find this warning from God, in response to the complaints of the Israelites:

'Why have we fasted, and thou
seest it not?

Why have we humbled ourselves,

and thou takest no knowledge

of it?'

Behold, in the day of your fast you

seek your own pleasure,

and oppress all your workers.

Behold, you fast only to quarrel and

to fight

and to hit with your wicked fist.

Fasting like yours this day

will not make your voice to be

heard on high.

Is such the fast that I choose,

a day for a man to humble

himself?

Is it to bow down his head like a rush

and to spread sackcloth and ashes

under him?

Will you call this a fast,

and a day acceptable to the Lord? (Isa 58:3-5)

Fasting is more than a physical practice; it is an act of the heart. Fasting must lead to deeper humility and increased self-control. If it does not, then we must repent and try again.

Fasting then is a sacrifice we make in love to God: "I appeal to you therefore, brethren, by the mercies of God, to present your bodies as a living sacrifice, holy and acceptable to God, which is your spiritual worship" (Rom.

12:1). St. John Chrysostom, commenting on this passage, states:

> And how is the body, it may be said, to become a sacrifice? Let the eye look on no evil thing, and it has become a sacrifice; let your tongue speak nothing filthy, and it has become an offering; let your hand do no lawless deed, and it has become a burnt offering....let the hand do alms, the mouth bless those who cross us, and the hearing find leisure evermore for lections of Scripture.[3]

When fasting our whole self should participate. To fast is much more than to avoid certain foods. We must also avoid evil and sinful practices. Further, we pray and practice works of charity with time and resources that are acquired through our "giving up."

Again, fasting, although an important practice in the Church, should not be viewed legalistically. Legalism reduces ascetical practice to pharisaical pride. We should begin in moderation and slowly work toward the ideal, practiced in monasteries. Like any other work, fasting requires practice. As we grow in our practice, though we will sense a liberation. Tito Colliander writes, "Altogether too much of one's thoughts are taken up with care for sustenance and the enticements of the palate; one wishes to be free from them. Thus fasting is a step on the road to emancipation and an indispensable support in the struggle against selfish desires."[4]

When our minds are not occupied with satisfying our fleshly desires, we find more time to contemplate God and His wonderful creation. Moreover, our minds become clearer when our stomach is not full.

> One should not ponder divine matters on a full stomach.... When the stomach is constricted, the heart is humbled. He who fasts prays with a sober mind, but the mind of the intemperate person is filled with impure fancies and thoughts..... The vigil of groping thought is replaced by a vigil of clarity; troublesome searching is changed to quiet acceptance in gratitude and humility.[5]

Many of the Fathers teach that we should conclude our meal as soon as our hunger subsists, never eating until we are completely full.

Thus fasting should be viewed as a means to humility and self-control. It consists in more than not eating at all or avoiding certain foods; we must also fast from all sin and evil practices. Of course, this is not to say that we can be lax concerning sinful actions during non-fasting times. We should view periods of fasting (such as Great Lent or the Nativity fast) as a training camp, a time to become more aware of what is important and what is not; a time to focus on our life with God; a time to strengthen ourselves in the spiritual warfare of the Christian life. We must remember too that fasting is not just negation, but it should include good works and the practice of the virtues. A good way of practicing charity during a fast is to give to the poor the food we do not eat, or the extra money we would have spent on our meals.

Through fasting and a life of moderation, we will become more disciplined and self-controlled. In doing so, we will move further along the path to purity.

Prayer

Much has been written regarding prayer. It is at the heart of Orthodox spirituality. While the Church prescribes times for fasting, prayer is to be practiced at all times. "Pray without ceasing" (I Thes 5:17). So rich are the Orthodox teachings on prayer that it would be impossible to summarize in such a short space. What we can do, however, is learn some helpful practices and suggestions that can deepen our prayer life. For without prayer there is no spiritual growth, much less purity of heart.

Prayer is a weapon in the spiritual warfare we are called to fight each day. Not only are we called to pray without ceasing, but we are called to make our lives, everything we think, do, and say, a prayer to God. Many of the Holy Fathers have written on the importance of prayer and how it is to permeate into every area of our existence. Within the Patristic tradition we have no shortage of inspirational writings about the practice of prayer. *The Philokalia*, *The Art of Prayer*, and *Unseen Warfare* are but a few of the important works that can be found in the treasure chest of Orthodox spirituality. From this rich tradition we can explore some helpful advice in developing a deeper prayer life.

First, we must develop our own prayer rule. In monastic settings the faithful still keep the hours of the Church. Vespers, done in the evening at sunset, opens the daily cycle; Compline is said before sleep; Nocturnes is the midnight service; Matins is performed at sunrise, followed by the first hour (7:00am); third hour (9:00am); sixth hour (noon); and ninth hour (3:00pm). While we may be unable to pray all the hours of the Church, we must still establish certain periods of the day for prayer. We must keep our rule and not be too flexible with it. If we let the cares of the world dictate when we pray and when we ignore our prayer rule, we will likely find our prayer time becoming increasingly infrequent and might disappear altogether.

A prayer rule is an important discipline in the Christian life. It gives us definite times for prayer and brings a steady rhythm to our often chaotic lives. Further, it *forces* us to pray. Without a prayer rule, our prayer life will be sporadic and our spiritual life will be filled with needless "peaks and valleys." St. John of Kronstadt writes, "If you pray only when you are inclined to, you will cease praying altogether; this is what the flesh desires. *The kingdom of God suffereth violence.* You will not be able to work out your salvation without forcing yourself."[6]

To pray consistently and often is no easy task. St. John also offers these words of encouragement: "Learn to pray; force yourself to pray. In the beginning it will be difficult; but afterwards the more you force yourself to pray, the more easily you will do so. But in the beginning, it is always necessary to force oneself."[7] St. Innocent offers similar advice, adding that if we force ourselves, we will receive the gift of prayer.

> Pray, my friend, pray as much as you can. Force yourself to pray. The desire to pray is a gift from God and isn't always given. It is, however, inevitably to those who *force* themselves to pray that it is given. At first it seems burdensome and difficult, but becomes lighter and lighter as you go. Then, when you receive the gift of prayer you'll never desire anything greater.[8]

In other words, the more we pray, the more our desire to pray increases. More importantly, God rewards us with the gift of prayer: that is, where prayer becomes more natural; it flows from our very existence. This is not to say, however, that we will not experience dry periods or times when it is more difficult to pray; we will find, instead, that prayer is less difficult and throughout the day our minds and hearts will turn more frequently to God.

Once we establish a prayer rule, morning and evening prayers, for example, we must learn to pray in such a way that our words become spiritual incense before the throne of God. First, it is important that we believe not only in God but believe that He will answer our prayers: "And without faith it is impossible to please him. For whoever would draw near to God must believe that he exists and that he rewards those who seek him" (Heb 11:6). It may seem ridiculous to say that we must believe in God if we are already praying. Does not the mere act of prayer presuppose a belief in the existence of God? Yet how often do we pray without considering that we are speaking to the God of the universe? Proper preparation is important before addressing God in prayer. But it is not enough to believe *in* God; we must also believe that He hears our prayers and answers according to His good and perfect will (cf. Jas 2:19). Colliander states:

> Prayer is one wing, faith the other, that lifts us heavenward. With only one wing no one can fly: prayer without faith is as meaningless as faith without prayer. But if your faith is very weak, you can profitably cry: Lord, give me faith! Such a prayer seldom goes unheard.[9]

Like the gift of prayer, so too is faith a gift.

Prayer is essential to spiritual warfare. To pray is to be watchful, guarding our hearts and minds from the enemy. "Prayer and watchfulness are one and the same, for it is with prayer that you stand at the gate of your heart. The watchful eye reacts immediately to the slightest shifting in the field of vision; so also does the heart that is steadfast."[10] Thoughts, not always sinful ones, will enter our minds during prayer and distract us from what we are saying. Particularly disturbing are thoughts that plague us during the Divine Liturgy. Our minds often drift to our afternoon plans and projects, work, family, or, if we have been fasting, we often think of food. While it is impossible to pray without such distractions, we must continually refocus, gently dispelling the thoughts and returning to the words we are praying. If we were in the presence of a great world figure would we think about lunch or what we will do when we get home? How much more then should we be reverent and attentive during our prayer and the services of the Church. It is not without reason that the priest (or deacon) cries out: "Let us be attentive."

Such an effort is obviously difficult work, work that can never be ignored. When our lips are saying one thing and our minds are on another we are not truly praying. "To leave off praying is the same thing as deserting one's post. The gate stands open for the ravaging hordes, and the treasures one has gathered are plundered."[11] Prayer then requires our full attention. Not only must we concentrate on what we are saying, but we must also guard our hearts and minds at all times, so that the enemy is unable to enter. We must remember that any intrusive thought must be abandoned. While it is obvious that blatantly evil thoughts (lust, fantasies, and judging others, for example) should be dismissed, but so should the seemingly good thoughts that the enemy can place in our minds to distract us from our true purpose. (The enemy in such cases could be the flesh or actual demonic activity, or a combination of both.)

Being on guard then should be practiced at all times during prayer, whether alone or in our parishes. Watchfulness and faith, as well as love, allow us to pray effectively, according to Orthodox teachings. What is conspicuously absent are so-called spiritual experiences. It is not that spiritual experiences are lacking in the Lives of the Saints. One has to look no further than St. Seraphim of Sarov or St. Symeon the New Theologian to discredit that belief. Yet, during our prayer time, we do not seek spiritual experiences, rather we soberly seek God and entrust ourselves into His consistent compassion toward us and those we love, and surrender ourselves to His will for us. Moreover, we are taught that it is wrong to seek spiritual experiences. To seek such experiences or "ecstasy" is to open ourselves to what is known as *prelest* or spiritual deception. The "goal" of prayer is to be sober-minded. Metropolitan Anthony Bloom writes,

> The early Fathers and the whole Orthodox tradition teach us that we must concentrate, by an effort of will, on the prayer we pronounce. We must pronounce the words attentively, matter of factly, without trying to create any sort of emotional state, and we

must leave it to God to arouse whatever response we are capable of.[12]

Hence, saying our prayers attentively and with faith is necessary; the exalted emotional states are not.

Second, our morning and evening prayers are essential, but prayer does not stop here. We must maintain a prayerful heart throughout the day, pausing during our busy schedules to offer a prayer to God. The Jesus Prayer ("Lord Jesus Christ, Son of God, have mercy on me, a sinner") is perfect for hectic lives. It is short yet powerful. Whether we are walking to our car, going to lunch, or simply finding a few moments in between tasks, we can say the Jesus Prayer. By doing so we are constantly drawing our hearts and minds to God. Many of the Fathers taught that the remembrance of God is itself a prayer.

Our prayer rule is but a frame that holds the picture, our daily lives, in place. We rise in the morning and pray; we continue throughout the day to remember God, to offer brief prayers to Him; then we close the day with prayers of thanksgiving and confession of our sins. St. John of Kronstadt writes,

> The only means by which you can spend the day in perfect holiness, and peace, and without sin, is more sincere prayer as soon as you rise from sleep in the morning.... Never sleep before saying evening prayers, lest your heart become gross from ill-timed sleep, and lest the enemy hinder it by a stony insensibility during prayer.[13]

Many of us may think our mornings are too rushed and chaotic as it is, without adding a time for prayer. To this St. John responds, "Get up earlier, pray diligently and you will acquire tranquility, energy and success at work, for the whole day."[14]

Prayer books are useful for enhancing our prayer life. Many of them contain the prayers and psalms for the different hours of the day. A good prayer book should include the morning and evening prayers. By praying the psalms and the prayers of the saints, our hearts are molded and deepened so that our prayer times are also instructional times. Praying the prayers of the Church is an excellent way to learn the faith and how to pray more effectively. St. Theophan the Recluse encourages us to use prayer books, for they contain the prayers of the holy fathers: Saint Ephraim the Syrian, Saint Macarius of Egypt, Saint Basil the Great, Saint John "Golden Mouth" Chrysostom and the other great masters of prayer. As they were themselves filled with the spirit of prayer, they put words to what the spirit revealed to them, and they passed it on to us. Thus a great power of prayer moves in their every prayer. By the law of reciprocal action, those who enter energetically and attentively into these prayers will taste the power of the original prayer to the extent that their spirit comes close to the spirit it contains. [15]

In short, prayer books deepen our prayer life by helping us enter into the spirit in which they were written.[16]

As we develop a consistent prayer rule, our spirituality will deepen. Also prayer purifies our hearts and minds:

[Prayer] purifies the mind of evil and wicked thoughts. However, with time purification takes place in both [the intellect and the heart] simultaneously....The more the heart becomes purified, the more the intellect becomes enlightened. The more the intellect is purified, the more the heart shines.[17]

Through prayer we are cleansed, purified, and transformed.

St. Theophan the Recluse offers us some good practical advice, concerning prayer.[18] His teachings on prayer are vast, but three suggestions help in deepening our prayer lives. First, we are told to prepare ourselves by quieting our hearts and minds, focusing on the awesome act we are about to perform: speaking directly to the Lord of the universe, the Creator of "all things visible and invisible." He writes,

> So, morning or evening, immediately before you begin to repeat your prayers, stand awhile, sit for a while, or walk a little and try to steady your mind and turn it away from all worldly activities and objects. After this, think who He is to whom you turn in prayer, then recollect who you are; who it is who is about to start this invocation to Him in prayer. Do this in such a way as to wake in your heart a feeling of humility and reverent awe that you are standing in the presence of God.[19]

We should not rush into His presence. By quieting ourselves and remembering Who it is we are addressing, our minds become more focused and our hearts more contrite.

As we begin to pray, we should pay attention to what we are saying. "Simply enter in to every word and then bring the meaning of each word down into your heart. That is, understand what you say, and then experience what you have understood."[20] Our understanding cannot be enlightened, nor will our hearts be transformed, if we fail to concentrate on the words being said. The prayers of the Church are not magical, in that all we have to do is repeat them and then we will become holy. The prayers that our Holy Fathers have handed down to us are tools or means to reach our ultimate goal: communion with God. They teach us how to pray and how we should approach God. But simply repeating them mindlessly without attention does little good and could even be harmful if we think that in doing so we are fulfilling our obligation to God.

At the same time, however, we must realize that our minds will wander. Nonetheless, we simply refocus, bringing our thoughts back to God and to the words we are speaking. Our hearts at times will also experience coldness, when the words seem meaningless and our prayer seems dry. But again we must struggle to utter the words with feeling and attention, taking time to confess to God the state in which we find ourselves. For Christ knows our struggle and our temptations and is willing to help us overcome them (cf. Heb 2:18). The psalmists certainly knew what it was like to experience dry periods (see Ps 42, for example). Often, as we pray our hearts will slowly warm, and we begin praying from the depths of our being.

Third, St. Theophan encourages us to "ease out" of prayer just as we entered it. We quiet ourselves before we pray, and having finished, we do the same before entering into our daily activities (or before going to sleep). He writes that "once you have finished saying your prayers, do not immediately go on to do something else. Stand for awhile and consider what it is to which all this commits you. Try to hold in your heart what has been given you to feel during prayer."[21] Take a few moments to recollect what has just taken place. If certain phrases from the psalms or prayers stand out, then meditate on them for a moment. How will I apply these words in my life? St. Theophan states, "Nobody who has fulfilled his rule of prayer with care will immediately want to return to his ordinary interests. This is the quality of true prayer!"[22] Anyone having finished his or her prayer rule and then goes to the living room and turns on the television knows the truth of this statement. It is like an unpleasant dip into a cold pool.

Finally, it should be added that a prayer rule is a part of our life in the Church. Even our private prayers should not be viewed as something we do as individuals. Our private prayers augment, enhance, and supplement our corporate prayers. Fr. Alexander Schmemann writes that "the division between 'corporate' and 'private' worship must be discarded. The purpose of worship is to constitute the Church, precisely to bring what is 'private' into the new life, to transform it into what belongs to the Church, i.e. shared with all in Christ."[23] In order to pray well at Church we must pray well at home. One cannot separate private and corporate prayers any more than an athlete can separate training from the actual sporting event. Without one, the other fails to exist.

We see therefore that our private prayers prepare us for corporate prayers. Moreover, we never really pray privately. We believe that we are surrounded by "a great cloud of witnesses" (Heb 12:1). Further, when we pray the hours, we pray with monks, nuns, and other believers throughout the world. Our prayer lives deepen, by praying, by practicing our prayer rule, by praying in communion with the Church, by living a life of prayer. If we desire to obtain purity of heart, our lives must become a prayer. This happens only when we establish a life of prayer.

Almsgiving

Almsgiving and acts of charity make up the "third leg" of our three-legged stool of Christian spirituality. Through the lives and teachings of the saints we find many examples of acts of charity. Further, Scripture is clear in instructing, even warning, us that almsgiving is not an option. With these admonitions from the saints and from Scripture in mind, it behooves the Orthodox Church of contemporary North America to make a more concerted effort in reaching out to those around her. We need to consider the roots of our faith and become active in loving and caring for others. Unfortunately, we have chosen to live in isolation, nostalgic ethnicity, and lethargic comfort rather than living more fully the Gospel. It is not enough to quote the Fathers and bask in our rich Tradition and contend how we have maintained the ancient faith. It is certainly true that the Orthodox Church has preserved the faith, even under much pressure and oppression, but let us not forget the words of St. James:

> What does it profit, my brethren, if a man says he has faith but has not works? Can his faith save him? If a brother or sister is ill-clad and in lack of daily food, and one of you says to them, "Go in peace, be warmed and filled," without giving them the things needed for the body, what does it profit? So faith by itself, if it has no works, is dead. (Jas 2:14-17)

It is not enough for us to abstain from food and pray for others. What we do not eat should go to the poor; those for whom we pray should be given help in whatever way we can. St. Basil the Great writes:

> The bread you do not use is the bread of the hungry. The garment hanging in your wardrobe is the garment of the person who is naked. The shoes you do not wear are the shoes of the one who is barefoot. The money

you keep locked away is the money of the
poor. The acts of charity you do not perform
are the injustices you commit.

These are strong words. While we speak of being the
Church of the early Fathers, how many of us can claim that
we live the lives of the Fathers or even follow their
teachings? Likewise, with such a rich treasure of teachings
and examples, will we not be held accountable for having
such a gift and doing so little with it? The words of Christ
give us a clear warning:

> And that servant who knew his master's will,
> but did not make ready or act according to
> his will, shall receive a severe beating. But he
> who did not know, and did what deserved a
> beating, shall receive a light beating. Every
> one to whom much is given, of him will
> much be required; of him to whom men
> commit much they will demand the more.
> (Luke 12:47-48)

This example must make serious Christians consider how
well they are applying what they know. We have been
handed down a rich heritage; if, however, we fail to share
and live what we know, we must repent and return to the
faith of our Fathers.

In order to understand the mind of the Church concerning almsgiving, let us first look at the Scriptural teaching on this subject.[24] In the book of Deuteronomy, we find clear instruction about how we are to treat the poor.

> If there is among you a poor man, one of your brethren, in any of your towns within your land which the Lord your God gives you, you shall not harden your heart or shut your hand against your poor brother, but you shall open your hand to him, and lend him sufficient for his need, whatever it may be.... You shall give to him freely, and your heart shall not be grudging when you give to him; because for this the Lord your God will bless you in all your work and in all that you undertake. For the poor will never cease out of the land; therefore I command you. You shall open wide your hand to your brother, to the needy and to the poor, in the land. (Deut 15:7-8, 10-11)

Not only were they to give to their "brethren," they were to make provisions for the sojourner, the fatherless, and the widow:

> When you reap your harvest in your field, and have forgotten a sheaf in the field, you shall not go back to get it; it shall be for the sojourner, the fatherless, and the widow. When you beat your olive trees, you shall not go over the boughs again; it shall be for the sojourner, the fatherless, and the widow. (Deut 24:18-20)

Again, we find a similar passage in Leviticus: "And when you reap the harvest of your land, you shall not reap your field to its very border, nor shall you gather the gleanings after your harvest; you shall leave them for the poor and for the stranger: I am the Lord your God" (Lev. 23:22). What is striking about these passages is that, first, they are not mere suggestions, but commandments; second, the poor, the stranger, the widow, and the fatherless were to receive help, not based on their character or how they might use what they receive, but because of their condition. In fact, by leaving the gleanings after harvest, the worker would not necessarily see who took what remained, making

115

it difficult for any value judgment to be cast upon the person.

The prophets had much to say about the treatment of the poor. They decried the amassing of wealth, while ignoring the poor. The Lord said through His prophet Jeremiah that the wicked "have grown fat and sleek" but they "judge not with justice the cause of the fatherless," nor do they "defend the rights of the needy" (Jer 5:27-28). In the same manner, Amos tells the Israelites that God will not revoke punishment because they trampled "the head of the poor into the dust of the earth" (Amos 2:7).

Fasting and giving alms are closely tied together. During periods of fasting, we should make time for good works, for almsgiving. The Lord, speaking through Isaiah, told the Israelites:

> Is this not the fast that I choose: to loose the bonds of wickedness, to undo the thongs of the yoke? Is it not to share your bread with the hungry, and bring the homeless poor into your house; when you see the naked to cover him, and not hide yourself from your own flesh? (Isa 58:6-7)

When the two, almsgiving and fasting, are done together, the Lord promises that your light shall "break forth like the dawn, and your healing shall spring up speedily," and "the glory of the Lord shall be your rear guard"(Isa 58:8). It is then that the Lord promises that He will hear our cry.

The New Testament teaching on giving to the poor is less systematic than what we find in the Old Testament. No longer do we find certain rules prescribing how much to give or at what time of the year or to whom. We are to give freely, for freely we have received (cf. Matt 10:8). Our "harvest" is not all that is required; instead we are to give of our wages, our possessions, and our time. In short, we are to give of ourselves, making our very lives sacrifices unto God.

A few examples of the New Testament teaching on giving show the radical nature of the Christian teaching. The Forerunner, St. John the Baptist, when asked, "What shall we do?" answered: "He who has two coats, let him share with him who has none; and he who has food, let him do likewise" (Luke 3:10). The words of Christ spoken to the rich young ruler are even more difficult: "If you would be perfect, go, sell what you possess and give to the poor, and you will have treasure in heaven; and come, follow me" (Matt 19:21). While it would be impossible for everyone to sell everything and give to the poor, it is the ideal, an ideal that finds its fulfillment in monasticism. We need money to feed our families, to support the Church, the monasteries, and charitable organizations. Yet the statement strikes at the core of our personal lives: How willing are we to give up everything for the Kingdom of God? Are we willing to give, even beyond what we think we can afford, in order to help the poor and needy? Are we willing to consume less and live modestly so that others may be more comfortable? to use money within our churches to support missions and to reach out to the poor in our communities instead of hoarding money or using it to build ethnic centers or gymnasiums? In short, are we willing, in the words of Gandhi, to "live simply so that others may simply live?"

Christ also taught us to give to all who ask of us: "Give to everyone who begs from you; and of him who

takes away your goods do not ask them again" (Luke 6:30).
Note that no mention is made concerning the recipient's
worthiness. Much like the Old Testament passages quoted
previously, these words have no qualifications or moral
criteria attached to them. Christ tells us to *give*, when asked.
St. Maximus the Confessor offers a similar teaching:

> He who gives alms in imitation of God does
> not discriminate between the wicked and the
> virtuous, the just and the unjust, when
> providing for men's bodily needs. He gives
> equally to all according to their need, even
> though he prefers the virtuous man to the
> bad man because of the probity of his
> intention.

While we would like to think that the money, food, or
clothing that we give will be used wisely and appropriately,
we cannot wait until we have that assurance. Again, we are
told to give, not to make moral judgments or ask of the
recipient that a certain criteria be met before receiving our
alms. (It should be added that many missions and outreach
services require that the person do some task or certain
amount of work in order to obtain groceries and clothing.
Such projects are good and beneficial when done in love.

The recipient senses that the "alms" were earned, taking away some of the shame that many feel in such situations. Regardless, the moral "worth" of the person is not a condition.)

Almsgiving should be done by the body of Christ as a corporate act of charity. Each individual member, however, must also practice these acts of love in his or her daily life. There should be no dichotomy between our individual acts and our corporate ones (except perhaps that the former is done on a smaller scale).

In our everyday lives we may practice almsgiving in many ways. Finding a good charity to support is one way. Another is to keep our ears and eyes open to those whose needs may or may not be expressed overtly. Such awareness precludes our preoccupation with the self: our plans, daydreams, and worries. Many who live and work in big cities are approached often by those who are asking for money. These encounters are the cause of much uncertainty in many well-meaning people. Often the person is rude, demanding, and may make a living by panhandling.

Further, the same person might use the money for alcohol or drugs. While discernment is necessary in such incidents, it is better to err on the side of compassion than on the side of cynicism. In doing so, we learn to let go of our possessions and to experience the freedom of not clinging so tightly to something as transient as money. Besides, a dollar or two is not a huge sacrifice, yet this small sacrifice often does more for us than for the beggar receiving our alms.

Christ said that we are to give and not expect repayment. When practicing this precept we not only give to the one who asks but we learn to be more detached from "manna." As Christians, God asks us to trust that He will meet our needs and provide what is necessary. By giving away money and possessions, we learn to give of ourselves, to die to our own materialism, our wants and desires. And this is not easy. St. Macarius states, "In coming to the Lord, a man must force himself to do that which is good, even against the inclination of his heart, continually, expecting His mercy with undoubting faith, and force himself to love when he has no love."

As for those to whom we may not want to give, St. Isaac the Syrian offers this advice:

> When you give, give generously, with a joyous countenance, and give more than you are asked for.... Do not separate the rich from the poor, nor try to discriminate the worthy from the unworthy, but let all men be equal in your eyes for a good deed. In this way you can draw even the unworthy toward the good, since the soul is easily led to the fear of God by bodily things. The Lord ate at a table with publicans and harlots and did not alienate the unworthy, that He might in this way bring all to the fear of God, and that through bodily things they would approach the spiritual.[25]

He also warns: "The poor and indigent man is provided for by God (because God abandons no one); but as for you, you have shunned the honour given you by God and have estranged His grace from you by turning a beggar away."[26]

Ignoring the distinctions between good and bad, rich and poor, worthy and unworthy, is, as we have already seen, moving beyond the surface and into the world of the pure of heart. It is worth repeating that each person—whether it be a drug addict, prostitute, alcoholic, or panhandler—is created in the image of God. It is God's purpose for that person to grow in His likeness. Thus we must love all people, not for what we see, but for who they are.

While giving alms is required of each Christian, we must be aware of the two-fold danger that can arise in doing this act of love. First, much like fasting or any virtue, giving to the needy can cause us to become hypocritical or prideful. Pride manifests itself in two ways: the desire to be noticed by others, even thanked by the recipient; and also in our own condescending attitude toward those who ask us for alms. Christ addressed this first problem:

> Thus, when you give alms, sound no trumpet before you, as the hypocrites do in the synagogues and in the streets, that they may be praised by men. Truly, I say to you, they have received their reward. But when you give alms, do not let your left hand know what your right hand is doing, so that your alms may be in secret; and your Father who sees in secret will reward you. (Matt 6:2-4)

No matter how strong the temptation we must give quietly and covertly.

Many times in our parishes we are asked to make donations for a certain project. It has become an Orthodox practice, albeit not necessarily a Christian one, to honor the contributors by putting their name on a plaque at the bottom of an icon or in the parish newsletter. This is a "tradition" that seems to fly in the face of Christ's teachings. Although this practice is widely used, it would be good for us to donate anonymously. In doing so, "your Father who sees in secret will reward you."

Another danger has to do with our attitude toward those to whom we give. In any social contact there can be a vying for superiority. Who is the most powerful? Who is the smartest? The scales can tip in different directions with the same two people, depending on the situation. When someone approaches us asking for money, there is no question about who has the upper hand (although the use of intimidation by some panhandlers reverses the scenario). We can too easily whip out a few dollars, push it into the person's hand, while thinking, "Why doesn't he just get a job?" or "Why doesn't she just quit using drugs and alcohol?" In some cases these attitudes are just as tangible as the small sum we place in the poor person's hand. St. Dorotheos of Gaza teaches that our act of giving "is perfect when a man gives alms without meanness or reluctance, without despising the recipient but with eagerness according to his ability, of deliberate choice, giving as freely as if he were receiving, doing a kindness as graciously as if a kindness were being shown to him."[27] This attitude conveys a certain "childlikeness," an innocence free of the cynicism of our times.

If each person is responsible to give alms, how much more so should we, when called together and acting as the body of Christ, give to the poor? It should be clear now that this virtue is not an option. Giving to the poor is a basic Christian act that cannot be ignored, regardless of how little it may be practiced in our own Church life. Any Christian should need no convincing that this is true. But it is helpful to see what almsgiving is *not*.

In our modern age we see all kinds of Christian activism that promote social justice and civil liberties but myopically and ironically, keep the Gospel secret rather than their giving. Their failure to effectively transform lives leads many to feel confused or skeptical about the Church's role in helping the poor. Moreover, we have watched governments begin their own form of "almsgiving." Unfortunately, these, too, have proved ineffective in transforming lives. While many argue that government help serves only to degrade the recipient and perpetuate the problem, others criticize the Christian activism approach that appears too often as an attempt to build a man-made kingdom of God, an approach that is far from "other worldly" and more closely resembles secular social services.

While it would be impossible to enumerate the various problems and contradictions that exist with both secular social services and the Social Gospel movement, certainly one problem that is obvious is the limitation of their vision. Both seek to transform society, not persons. While it is excusable, if not predictable, that government social services would fall prey to such delusions, it is less understandable when Christians do the same. Both attempt to "heal" the ills of society, while disregarding the unique problems of each person. They therefore fail to offer Christ

Himself, and substitute in His place "worldly bread" for the bread of the world.

We see this tragedy at its worst with government agencies that purport to help the needy. What is usually the case is that a person will go to apply for help, answer some questions dished out in a routine manner by an over-worked social worker, who may or may not bother to look the applicant in the eyes; and then the person is told whether or not he or she meets the criteria. While many of the people who work in these settings are well meaning and sincere, they find themselves in a system that does not allow them to love, to help, or to offer what the person truly needs. They are bogged down with endless paper work and large caseloads that preclude any real help. Secular social services have tried to provide bread, but we do not live by bread alone. It is not surprising, then, that these agencies are, for the most part, unable to change the lives of those they serve. For any program that does not operate on the foundation of love and the belief that we— both giver and recipient—are created in the image of God is doomed to failure. Each person must be seen as unique, with problems and needs, as well as talents and dreams. If we lose sight of this "uniqueness," we end up with the scenario created by Dostoevsky in "The Grand Inquisitor" and in his novel *The Possessed*, where we find men whose so-called love for humanity is so great they eventually hate the person. They see only the masses who need their help but despise anyone who may disagree with their idealism.

The Social Gospel practiced in a number of denominations and philanthropic organizations commits a similar error. At the root of these ministries is an implied, if not an explicit, belief that society can be perfected by humans. Again, the emphasis is on the masses, and the means are largely material. Elder Ambrose of Optina states, "Moral perfection on earth (which is imperfect) is not attained by mankind as a whole but rather by the individual believer according to the degree to which he fulfills God's commandments and the degree of his humility."[28]

What is so disheartening is that these ministries have secularized their services. Instead of modeling their outreach after the Kingdom of God, they have copied the paradigm of the secular social services. An evident manifestation of this is seen in their "bigger must be better" attitude. Fr. Seraphim Rose saw this discrepancy and pointed out the well-meaning but "this worldly" formula: If feeding one person is good, how much better would it be to feed a thousand? Fr. Seraphim reminds us and all who are tempted to engage in this Social Gospel that

> Christ did not come to feed the hungry, but to save the souls of all, hungry or replete. When we see a hungry man, it is not some mechanical sense that is affected within us; we do not say, "Here is another one to be fed," and immediately calculate the stores of food available—or, if we do this, our soul is dead, capable of counting but not loving man. No, it is our heart that is touched, for here is man, hungry and naked as I, even as our God when He came among us; here is a man. If Christ be truly in our hearts, it is a matter of course that we give this man what we have; but if we have nothing, our love is not therefore the less. In fact, the less we have, the more likely it is that we will respond to this man as a human being.[29]

In short, we love the person who is in need. We give what we can give, always remembering that ultimate goal—the reason for which all humanity was created—is communion with God, the redemption of our souls. The bigger our ministry becomes, the less chance that the individual will be treated according to his or her unique circumstances.

Jesus said, "For truly, I say to you, whoever gives you a cup of water to drink because you bear the name of Christ, will by no means lose his reward" (Mark 9:41). He did not say we are to create a program that will manufacture cups of water *en masse*. What Christ has called us to do is much simpler than that. We are to love, and because of our love we should give, give of our possessions and of ourselves. We are not called to model the secular programs that the government and other agencies have created. Nor are we called to create similar social programs for the poor, programs that put food on their table but leave their souls impoverished and neglected. Vigen Guroian correctly states: "It is not the business of the Church to impose a new, presumably more just, ethic of power on the world. Rather, it is the calling of the people of God to demonstrate his love for the world through their obedient service to his kingdom."[30] In other words, the

Kingdom of God is not of this world; we are not called to create a pseudo-kingdom based on secular premises and practices.

Does this mean that we should abandon all projects and wait for the needy to knock on our parish doors? Of course not. What it does mean is that when we set out to help others in whatever form (fund raising, missions, and projects) that we do so out of love and our desire to further the Kingdom, which will *not* have its fulfillment until the age to come. Orthodox outreaches such as soup kitchens, youth centers, and group homes are badly needed and conspicuously absent from the North American landscape. They should be manifestations of our community of love, our local parishes. Having said this we must keep in mind that starting an outreach is not the goal of the Church, but an outcome that grows out of the transformed lives in our parishes. Fr. Seraphim Rose writes, "The only 'social responsibility' of a Christian is to live, wherever and with whomever he may be, the life of faith, for his own salvation and as an example to others. If, in doing so, we help to ameliorate or abolish a social evil, that is a good thing—but that is not our goal."[31] Again, our goal is to participate fully in the life of the Church: prayer, fasting, almsgiving, confession and penance, and communion with God through the Holy Mysteries.

No matter how small the parish, outreach is essential. Even if it is a closet full of canned goods for those in the community, we are manifesting our love to those in need. Some will argue that their parishes are too small to do anything but pay bills and survive. Yet if we want to reach those around us and draw others into the fullness of the faith, we will have to get out of this self-preservation mode. We must look closely at how we are manifesting the body of Christ in our communities, not that we may transform the community but that we may lead others to the One who transforms lives.

The challenge for the Orthodox Church is a great one. Clergy and laity alike need to look honestly at the American culture and then ask, how can we bring the message of the Gospel to this land of hedonism and materialism? The answer does not lie in bake sales or new ethnic centers; nor does it lie in our nationalism and foreign languages. The answer lies in the truth that Christ is in us and among us. And at each Liturgy the priest offers us communion with the living God, the true Bread of Life. Guroian writes,

> The Orthodox churches in America have failed to make the Lord's banquet compelling because they have made the eucharistic meal a privilege of independent ethnic cults (one can substitute social or economic class or race when appropriate for other churches) rather than the public expression of the virtues, values, character and hope of the Kingdom of God. The cults work strenuously at being ethnic Greek, Russian or Armenian, and ethnic in a respectably American fashion. The most noticeable meal which such churches offer is the annual food bazaar. And it is to this meal, not the heavenly banquet, to which those on the highways, streets and hedgepaths are invited.[32]

Ethnic festivals, in and of themselves, are fine. But if more energy is spent promoting our ethnic foods than the Bread of Life, our Eucharistic feast, then something has gone terribly wrong.

One of the greatest challenges for the Orthodox Church in America is to find a way to keep their rich traditions, while at the same time not alienating the American people who need to hear about the faith. Most Orthodox did not come to North America for the purpose of evangelizing. But now that Orthodoxy has arrived, it must find ways not only to reach the American people but to assimilate enough of the culture so that their own children will remain in the faith. Frank Schaeffer writes, "Because of clinging to the languages of the country of origin, many Orthodox Churches are even losing contact with their own children, or second and third generations effectively lost to the Church. They grow up knowing more about ethnic holidays and nationalist folklore than about the basics of Christian living."[33] The Orthodox Church is universal, catholic, not limited to nations. Schaeffer states:

The historical Orthodox Church became known for *reaching out*, not for looking inward. It evangelized huge portions of the globe; all of the Slavic nations, the whole Middle East, Alaska, huge tracts of Africa, Europe and Asia, including the world's greatest land mass: Russia. Yet in some American congregations today the petty maintenance of native languages, customs and national festivals, often seems to take precedence over welcoming outsiders, seeking new converts and, *most important of all, teaching the faithful the basic doctrines of Orthodox theology, worship, confession, and ascetic moral living.*[34]

This challenge is as important as it is dangerous. If the Orthodox fail to follow the examples of St. Innocent and Sts. Cyril and Methodius in bringing the faith to the people in a language that they can understand, then the Orthodox can expect to remain the best kept secret in North America. On the other hand, while some of American culture is good, much of it is bad. The assimilation process must be done with much prayer and discernment. The seduction of consumerism, materialism, and crass individualism is strong and cannot be underestimated. To embrace the culture as a whole would be of course a grave mistake. Elimination of the language barrier, however, so that people can hear and understand the faith, is a good starting point.

Our almsgiving therefore must consist of more than a few dollars and some can goods. Within the Church is the great treasure of the Christian faith. We are called to give of our possessions and of ourselves; at the same time, unlike secular social services and Social Gospel movements, we are to share the life-giving message of the Christian faith. The two are inseparable. The tragedy of our times is that they seldom are done together: one is emphasized at the expense of the other. Just as the Incarnation affects the whole person—body and soul—so too must our mission meet the needs of both.

It should be added that while fasting, prayer, and almsgiving are essential to our faith, they should not be seen as the "three easy steps" to purity of heart. Any systematic method to achieve such a goal should be viewed with suspicion. Nor should the three be viewed as separate virtues. They make up the whole. And that "whole" is the life in the Church: living the hourly, daily, weekly liturgical cycle of Church life, which includes fasting, prayer, almsgiving, as well as Confession, penance, and frequent partaking of the Eucharist. The life of our Lord is lived out through the liturgical year. The instructions of the saints and Holy Fathers presuppose a life in the Church. Without such life, there is no purity of heart. Christ instructs us: "Abide in me, and I in you. As the branch cannot bear fruit by itself, unless it abides in the vine, neither can you, unless you abide in me" (John 15:4).

5

The Dance

Purity of heart is tantamount to single-mindedness. To be single-minded is to live in the fullness of the Church through prayer, fasting, and almsgiving. It is to participate in the Eucharistic life. But it is possible to do all the right things and still be double-minded. When we are double-minded, we are unstable in all our ways (Jas 1:7-8). St. James exhorts us: "Cleanse your hands, you sinners, and purify your hearts, you men of double mind" (Jas 4:8).

We can do the right activities but for the wrong motives. And ironically sometimes the harder we try the worse we become. Thus, for the truly single-minded, there is a letting go, a peace that comes when we forget about *achieving* purity of heart and begin focusing on the God

139

Who is present in the moment, without neglecting our acts of love and worship.

Not surprisingly, the pure in heart find a contentment, a contentment that transcends their own life and circumstances. While they are certainly practicing the Christian life, they have let go of their ambition to be perfect and are resting in the faith that God is working in them and all around them. Sometimes we strive to be so holy that we burn out and become discouraged, largely because we are running on our own power. Often even our desire to be pure in heart has its roots in the need to be noticed and respected by others. We want to be seen as saints and holy people.

While it is a thin line, one that can easily be crossed, at some point, we must rest not only in our given circumstances but also in our own weaknesses and imperfections, without becoming complacent. Christ says to us: "Come to me, all who labor and are heavy laden, and I will give you rest. Take my yoke upon you, and learn from me; for I am gentle and lowly in heart, and you will find rest for your souls. For my yoke is easy, and my burden is light" (Matt 11:28-30).

Contentment can be of course a dangerous state. If we are so content that we no longer perform acts of love and worship, nor do we battle the enemy, we are in danger of losing our souls. St. Paul writes about another form of contentment: "There is great gain in godliness with contentment; for we brought nothing into the world, and we cannot take anything out of the world; but if we have food and clothing, with these we shall be content" (I Tim 6:6-8). Even while in prison Paul is able to say: "Not that I complain of want; for I have learned, in whatever state I am, to be content. I know how to be abased, and I know how to abound; in any and all circumstances I have learned the secret of facing plenty and hunger, abundance and want. I can do all things in him who strengthens me" (Phil 4:11-13).

Knowing that our lives are in the hands of God allows us not only to face our circumstances but also to have them transformed by God's grace. Such an attitude is found in St. Ignatius of Antioch. While on his way to Rome to be martyred, he wrote, "And now in chains I am learning to have no desires."[1] St. Ignatius was so certain of God's love for him, so convinced that he was in God and with God, that his outward circumstances could not smolder the flame in his heart. No longer was he concerned about his future plans or projects; no longer was he worried about his weaknesses and imperfections; no longer was he concerned how others viewed him. His desires had melted away. He knew the end was near, but he was alive to God's presence in that precise moment.

If we are to learn contentment we must be convinced that all that happens to us is allowed by our loving Father. A prayer that is attributed to the Optina Elders, as well as to Metropolitan Philaret of Moscow, states:

> *O Lord grant me with tranquility of soul to meet all that the coming day may bring.* Grant me to surrender myself completely to Thy holy will. *At every hour of this day guide and sustain me in all things. Whatsoever tidings I may receive in the course of the day, teach me to receive them with peace of soul and with the firm conviction that Thy holy will governs*

all. Govern Thou my thoughts and feelings in all my words and deeds. *In all unforeseen circumstances let me not forget that all are sent by Thee.* Teach me to act firmly and wisely without embittering and embarrassing others.

O Lord, grant me strength to bear the weariness of the coming day and all that it shall bring. Govern Thou my will and teach me to pray, to believe, to hope, to suffer, to forgive and to love. Amen. (Italics mine.)

This prayer breathes the spirit of contentment. Not only is it a prayer of surrender, but it is a prayer of acceptance, acceptance of all that comes our way, to bear it not with grumbling and complaining but as a gift from God.

Metropolitan Anthony (Bloom) teaches that each morning we should offer up the day to God. In doing so,

the day itself is also blessed by God. Doesn't this mean that everything that it contains, everything that happens to us during it is within the will of God? Believing that things happen nearly by chance is not believing in God. And if we receive everything that happens and everyone that comes to us in this spirit, we shall see that we are called to do the work of Christians in everything. Every encounter is an encounter in God and in his sight. We are sent to everyone we meet on our way, either to give or to receive sometime without even knowing it.[2]

Thus, nothing happens outside of God's will. Even the most irritating people and events that come to us are within God's will. Believing this means that we should see it as an encounter with God.

To live in such a way means that we must live fully in the present moment, being obedient to God in whatever our circumstances are at that time. Too often, we are lost in our own thoughts, daydreaming about the future or reminiscing about the past. We clutter our minds with rehearsed conversations and other fantasies that rob us of the moment. In doing so we miss God in the present. The "truly Orthodox person always has both feet firmly on the ground, facing whatever situation is right in front of him. It is in accepting given situations, which requires a loving heart, that one encounters God."[3] Such a life is a life of single-mindedness. The distractions of the world and of our own thoughts and desires succumb to the Kingdom of God, the awareness of His presence.

The pure in heart are always aware of the Kingdom of God that is in them and around them. For most of us, however, such an awareness must be practiced and lived out by faith. Fr. Anthony Coniaris writes:

> We are truly enveloped by God's presence constantly, but because it is not a physical presence but a spiritual one, we need to practice it throughout the day: to stop and remind ourselves that God is with us; to try to see Him everywhere about us; to try to capture daily the sense of His presence. If we try consciously to realize His nearness, we shall experience ever more powerfully His strengthening presence in our lives.... Practice the idea that God is with you, in you, and about you. Practice it until you feel His presence. It is by practicing the Presence that the Presence becomes real.[4]

In such a way, the day is sanctified. Sensing the presence of God is not for Sunday morning only; His presence must permeate every aspect of our existence: on our way to and from work; at the work place; in our homes. In short, we must remind ourselves that He is "everywhere present and filling all things."

Again, it must be stressed that we can only practice the presence of God if we are living fully in the moment. When we are at home, we must be fully at home; when we are at work, we must be fully at work; when we are at church, we must be fully at church. Too often, when we are at home we are plagued with the anxieties and concerns from our daily work. In other words, when we are at home we are not really at home. When we are at work, we are often thinking about what we will do that evening or weekend. We daydream about vacations, new homes, or perhaps missed opportunities in our past. We are anything but alive in the present.

Too often our routines numb us not just to God's presence but to life in general. The Catholic novelist, Walker Percy, wrote about "everydayness," a condition that causes us to go through our routines in a fog. H.L. Mencken once cynically wrote, "The basic fact about existence is not that it is a tragedy, but that it is a bore. It's not so much a war as an endless standing in line." Of course, the statement hardly expresses the Christian world-view; for most, however, it is feeling well known in the contemporary world. We have all faced the boredom and ennui of everyday life. In some ways, those feelings are more difficult to overcome than the tragedies we face. At least the tragedies wake us up. A more Christian outlook is expressed by the Catholic theologian Hans Urs von Baltasar: "The supreme Christian value is not the experience of transcendence but bearing the monotony of everyday life in faith, hope and love." Our worries, struggles, joys, and boredom are part of the journey.

Ironically, sometimes we think and worry about what God's will is for our life. While this is a good concern, it should not rob us of the present moment. If we are neglecting or only half-listening to our spouse or our children, we can be sure we are missing the will of God. God's desire for us is that we show love, kindness, and compassion to those we encounter. Too often while we wring our hands about what God's will is for us, we are too anxious to pay attention to our loved ones, or we overlook a person who is hurting and needs encouragement. God's calling for each person is different, but His will for us as a whole is quite simple: "to do justice, and to love kindness, and to walk humbly with your God" (Micah 6:8).

We have all heard stories of people who have begun successful ministries that reach thousands, but they never bother to reach their own families. Many sincere Christians want to do something big for God. Such a desire is commendable. But doing something little for God must not be ignored. When we become convinced that smaller is often better than bigger, we become free to live our lives with much more simplicity. Plenty of "ministries" exist for us to do in our everyday lives. Fr. Seraphim Rose taught:

> The Church of Christ is alive and free.... You are in Christ's Church whenever you uplift someone bent down in sorrow, or when you give alms to the poor, and visit the sick. You are in Christ's Church when you cry out: 'Lord, help me.' You are in Christ's Church when you are good and patient, when you refuse to get angry at your brother, even if he has wounded your feelings. You are in Christ's Church when you pray: 'Lord, forgive him.' When you work honestly at your job, returning home weary in the evening but with a smile on your lips; when you repay evil with love—you are in Christ's Church. Do

you not see, therefore, young friends, how close the Church of Christ is?[5]

Thus, we are to bring God and His love into every situation. Only by living in the present can we truly do God's will in each moment.

Such attentiveness also enhances our prayer life. We must pay close attention to the words we pray, saying them with faith and feeling. We must forget our concerns, our earthly cares, and remember that our prayer is all that is important at that moment. We must not concern ourselves with what we need to do when we are finished; instead, we must remind ourselves that the present moment is all we have and what we are doing prayer at that moment is all that matters.

A good way to practice attentiveness is to block out all the incoming thoughts and quiet our hearts. This is especially important before prayer or the Liturgy. But we must train our hearts and minds by practicing attentiveness throughout each day. Notice the sunrise as you drive into work or the sunset as you leave. Turn off the radio and consciously observe the world around you. While on your lunch hour, pay attention to the people who pass you, the buildings, the parks that are near. Listen to the noise or the silence that is around you. Observe the world in which God has placed you, always realizing that God is *here* and He is in each one who passes you on the street. You may be surprised at how difficult this is and how quickly our minds begin filling up with distractions. Yet the more we practice, the more aware of God's presence we will become.

One way of achieving a more mindful approach to our daily lives is to remember our own mortality. Nothing sobers us and brings our lives into perspective as does the remembrance of death. St. John Climacus teaches that the remembrance of death "produces freedom from daily worries and breeds constant prayer and guarding of the mind."[6] Our work, our projects, our plans, and our dreams are seen in a different light when we reflect on our own mortality. Not that such things are necessarily wrong or bad, but they are often less important than we realize or want to admit. We hear stories of men and women who are diagnosed with a terminal disease and are told that they have only a short time to live. Often such people say that they are more thankful for each moment, more mindful of those around them, more aware of what is really important in life. We too can become more conscious of the present if we remind ourselves that this day may be our last, that our life on this earth may end at any moment. The remembrance of death is not intended to depress or discourage us; on the contrary, it is a dose of reality, medicine that often cures our petty wants and desires, reminding us of what is truly important and what is not.

The remembering of death reminds us that we are not of this world, that we are only sojourners passing through. The people of God before us "were stoned, they were sawn in two, they were killed with the sword; they went about in skins of sheep and goats, destitute, afflicted, ill-treated—of whom the world was not worthy—wandering over deserts and mountains, and in dens and caves of the earth" (Heb 11:37-38). And this is the world in which we are called to live out the Christian life. The remembrance of death puts into perspective our plans and projects as well as our hope of the world to come.

With single-mindedness, we are called to pursue the Kingdom of God. Each moment of our lives, we must be aware of God's presence and act in obedience to His will. He has freed us to live in the "eternal now," to enjoy His presence and to love His creation. It is unnecessary to worry about His plan for us. His plan is before us at each moment. All we have to do is to love God and our neighbor, love those who are placed before us and enjoy the world in which God has placed us. In doing so, we sense the wonder of creation or what Thomas Merton calls "the cosmic dance."

> What is serious to man is often trivial in the sight of God. What in God might appear to us as "play" is perhaps what he Himself takes most seriously. At any rate the Lord plays and diverts Himself in the garden of His creation, and if we could let go of our own obsession with what we think is the meaning of it all, we might be able to hear His call and follow Him in His mysterious, cosmic dance. We do not have to go very far to catch echoes of that game, of that dancing. When we are alone on a starlit night; when by chance we see the migrating birds in autumn descending on a grove of junipers to rest and eat; when we see children in a moment when they are really

children; when we know love in our own hearts...at such times the awakening, the turning inside out of all values, the "newness," the emptiness and the purity of vision that make themselves evident, provide a glimpse of the cosmic dance

For the world and time are the dance of the Lord in emptiness. The silence of the spheres is the music of a wedding feast. The more we persist in misunderstanding the phenomena of life, the more we analyze them out into strange, finalities and complex purposes of our own, the more we involve ourselves in sadness, absurdity and despair. But it does not matter much, because no despair can alter the reality of things, or stain the joy of the cosmic dance which is always there. Indeed, we are in the midst of it, and it is in the midst of us, for it beats in our very blood, whether we want it to or not.

Yet the fact remains that we are invited to forget ourselves on purpose, cast our awful solemnity to the winds and join in the general dance.[7]

Merton tells us that we can let go and enjoy God's presence in creation: let go of our analyzing; let go of our compartmentalizing; let go of the need to be right. We are not relieved of our responsibility to make decisions; we are free, however, from the anxiety that comes from our lack of faith and trust that God will meet all our needs.

We are free to enjoy God's wonderful creation. We are free to see Him in ourselves, in others, and in nature. We do not have to get caught up in the "externals," as important as they might be. For God is with us. The choir may be off key; the priest may speak too long; the icons may be too "Western"; the service may have too much or too little English. But God is with us. And maybe if we quiet ourselves enough, we just might hear His voice or see His presence in those around us. For God is in us and He has surrounded us with His presence, if we can only prepare ourselves to see beyond the surface, with purity of heart.

Bibliography

Ch. 1

Toward a Transformed Vision

1. Quoted by Fr. Vincent Rossi. "Acquisition of the Holy Spirit: The Role of the Holy Spirit According to Orthodox Spirituality." *Epiphany* 12, no.4 (Summer Annual 1992): 11.

2. W. E. Vine. *An Expository Dictionary of New Testament Words.* (Old Tappan, New Jersey: Fleming H. Revell Co.,1966), pp. 206-7.

3. See Matt. 15:18-20 and Luke 6:45.

4. Vine, pp. 231,183.

5. Thomas Merton. *The Inner Experience: Kinds of Contemplation (IV).* Offprint from *Cistercian Studies* Vol.xviii, 1983:4, p.298.

6. Gregory of Nyssa. *The Lord's Prayer, The Beatitudes.* Translated by Hilda C. Graef. *Ancient Christian Writers*, vol.18. (New York: Newman Press,1954), pp. 148-49.

7. Thomas Hopko. *All the Fulness of God.* (Crestwood, NY: St. Vladimir's Seminary Press,1982), p. 20.

8. Gregory Palamas. *The Trials.* Translated by Nicholas Gendle. (New York: Paulist Press,1983), p. 76.

9. Ibid., p. 76.

10. Quoted in Rossi, p. 19

11. Rossi makes this interesting comparison in the article mentioned above.

12. Timothy (Kallistos) Ware. *The Orthodox Church.* (New York: Penguin Books,1983), p. 217.

13. Timothy (Kallistos) Ware. *The Orthodox Way.* (Crestwood, New York: St. Vladimir's Seminary Press,1986), p. 169.

Ch. 2

The Human Person as Image and Likeness

1. Protopresbyter Michael Pomazansky. *Orthodox Dogmatic Theology.* (Platina, CA: St.   Herman of Alaska Brotherhood, 1983), pp. 137-8.
2. Archimandrite Kallistos Ware. *The Orthodox Way.* (Crestwood, NY: St. Vladimir's Seminary Press, 1986), p. 66.
3. Ware, p. 80.

4. Pomazansky, p. 122.

5. Pomazansky, p. 123.

6. Bishop Timothy (Kallistos)Ware. *The Orthodox Church.* (New York: Penguin Books, 1983), p. 225.

7. Pomazansky, pp. 136-7.

8. Ware. *The Orthodox Church,* pp. 225-6.

9. Gregory of Nyssa. *The Lord's Prayer, The Beatitudes.* Translated by Hilda C. Graef. *Ancient Christian Writers,* vol.18. (New York: Newman Press,1954), p. 149.

10. Pomazansky, p. 123.

11. Ibid., p. 124.

12. Christos Yannaras. *The Freedom of Morality*. (Crestwood, NY: St. Vladimir's Seminary Press, 1984), p. 31.

13. Ware, *The Orthodox Way*, p. 81.

14. Yannaras, p. 46.

15. Cal Thomas. "Conflict of the Two Kingdoms." *The Indianapolis Star*, July, 10, 1994, p. D2.

16. Georgios I. Mantzaridis. *The Deification of Man*. (Crestwood, NY: St. Vladimir's Seminary Press, 1984), p. 21.

17. Ware, *The Orthodox Church*, p. 237.

18. Ware, *The Orthodox Way*, p. 28.

19. Monk Damascene Christensen. *Not of This World: The Life and Teachings of Fr. Seraphim Rose*. (Forestville, CA: Fr. Seraphim Rose Foundation, 1993), p. 200.

20. See Ware, *The Orthodox Church*, pp. 240-2.

21. Ware, *The Orthodox Way*, p. 146.

Ch. 3

The Mystical Vision: Seeing Beyond the Veil

1. Gregory of Nyssa. *The Lord's Prayer, The Beatitudes*. Translated by Hilda C. Graef. *Ancient Christian Writers*, vol.18. (New York: Newman Press,1954), p. 145.

2. Ibid., pp.146-7.

3. Timothy (Kallistos) Ware. *The Orthodox Way*. (Crestwood, New York: St. Vladimir's Seminary Press, 1986), p. 31.

4.   Ibid., p. 58.

5.   Bishop Timothy (Kallistos) Ware. *The Orthodox Church*. (New York: Penguin Books, 1983), p. 217.

6.   Fyodor Dostoevsky. *The Brothers Karamozov*. Translated by Constance Garnett. The Norton Critical Edition. (New York: W. W. Norton and Co., 1976), p.298.

7.   Ware, *The Orthodox Way*, p. 29.

8.   "September 1: Protection of the Environment." *Solia*, Sept. 1993, p. 4.

9.   Brother Aiden. "Man and His Role in the Environment." *Epiphany* 12, no.4 (Summer Annual 1992): p.25.

10.   Ibid., p. 33.

11.   Ibid., p. 27.

12.   Quoted by Aiden, p.32.

13.   Quoted by Christos Yannaras. *The Freedom of Morality*. (Crestwood, NY: St. Vladimir's Seminary Press, 1984), pp. 271, 273.

14.   Quoted by Ware. *The Orthodox Church*, p. 226.

15.   Ware, *The Orthodox Way*, p. 70.

16.   Quoted by Ware. *The Orthodox Church*, p. 226.

17.   Gregory of Nyssa, p. 148.

18.   Thomas Hopko. *The Lenten Spring*. (Crestwood, NY: St. Vladimir's Seminary Press, 1983), p. 113.

19.   Ibid., p. 113.

20.   Ibid., p.114.

21.   Ibid., p.115.

22. *The Way of the Pilgrim and The Pilgrim Continues His Way.* Translated by R. M. French. (San Francisco: Harper and Row Publishers), p. 97.

23. Quoted by Ware. *The Orthodox Church*, p. 226

24. Thomas Merton. *The Inner Experience: Kinds of Contemplation (IV).* Offprint from *Cistercian Studies* Vol. xviii, 1983: 3, p.211.

25. Fr. Seraphim Rose. *The Heavenly Realm.* (Platina, CA: St. Herman of Alaska Brotherhood, 1984), p. 28.

26. Thomas Merton. *New Seeds of Contemplation.* (New York: New Directions, 1972), p. 296.

27. Ware, *The Orthodox Way*, p. 68.

Ch. 4

The Path to Purity

1. Rev. George Mastrantonis. *Fasting from Iniquities and Foods.* (St. Louis: OLOGOS), p. 6.

2. Stanley S. Harakas. *The Orthodox Church: 450 Questions and Answers.* (Minneapolis: Light and Life Publishing, 1987), p. 128.

3. *The Bible and the Holy Fathers for Orthodox.* Compiled and edited by Johanna Manley. (Menlo Park, CA: Monastery Books, 1990), p. 243.

4. Tito Colliander. *Way of the Ascetics.* (Crestwood, NY: St. Vladimir's Seminary Press, 1985), p.76.

5. Ibid., pp. 75-6.

6. Fr. John of Kronstadt. *Spiritual Counsels: Selected Passages from My Life in Christ.* Edited by W. Jardine Grisbrooke. (Crestwood, NY: St. Vladimir's Seminary Press, 1989), p. 47.

7. Ibid., p. 48.

8. Paul Garrett. *St. Innocent: Apostle to America.* (Crestwood, NY: St. Vladimir's Seminary Press, 1979), p. 218.

9. Colliander, p. 56.

10. Ibid., p. 58.

11. Ibid., p. 58.

12. Metropolitan Anthony (Bloom). *Living Prayer.* (Springfield, IL: Templegate Publishers, 1966), p. 59.

13. Fr. John of Kronstadt, pp. 13-14.

14. Bishop Alexander. *The Life of Father John of Kronstadt.* (Crestwood, NY: St. Vladimir's Seminary Press, 1979), p. 108.

15. St. Theophan the Recluse. *The Path of Prayer.* Translated by Ester Williams. Edited and compiled by Robin Amis. (Newbury, MA: Praxis Press, 1992), pp.1-2.

16. There are several good prayer books that are helpful in establishing a prayer rule: *A Manual of the Hours of the Orthodox Church* (Community of the Holy Myrrbearers, Otega, NY); *A Pocket Prayer Book for Orthodox Christians* (Antiochian Archdiocese); *Prayer Book* (Holy Trinity Mastery, Jordanville, NY); *Orthodox Prayer Book* (Mother Cassiana/Holy Protection Monastery); *The Hours of Prayer: A Book of Devotion* (The Orthodox Brotherhood of the Virgin Mary, Elkhorn, West Virginia).

17. Archimandrite IOANNIKIOS. *Themes from the Philokalia, No.1: Watchfulness and Prayer.*Translated by Jeanie E. Gentithes and Arch. Ignatios Apostolopoulos. (Minneapolis, MN: Light and Life Publishing, 1988), p. 59.

18. For a more thorough explanation of St. Theophan's teachings on prayer, as well as some helpful instruction from St. John of Kronstadt, see my *Flames of Wisdom: Spiritual Teachings for Daily Life.* (Indianapolis, IN: Theosis Books, 2016), chs. 3 and 4.

19. St. Theophan the Recluse, p. 3.

20. Ibid., p. 4.

21. Ibid., p. 7.

22. Ibid., p. 7.

23. Alexander Schmemann. *Introduction to Liturgical Theology.* Translated by Asheleigh E. Moorehouse. (Crestwood, NY: St. Vladimir's Seminary Press, 1986), p. 24.

24. Much of the information concerning the Old Testament teaching on our responsibility to the poor was taken from Richard J. Foster's *Freedom of Simplicity* (San Francisco: Harper and Row, 1981), pp. 15-32.

25. St. Isaac the Syrian. *The Ascetical Homilies of St. Isaac the Syrian.* Translated by Holy Transfiguration Monastery. (Boston: Holy Transfiguration Monastery, 1984), p. 37.

26. Ibid

27. Dorotheos of Gaza. *Discourses and Sayings.* Translated by Eric P. Wheeler. (Kalamazoo, MI: Cistercian Publications, 1977), p.208.

28. Quoted in *The Orthodox Word,* Vol. 22, No. 3 (128), May-June 1986; p. 125.

29. Eugene (Fr. Seraphim) Rose. "Christian Realism and Worldly Idealism." *The Orthodox Word* 22, no.3 (May-June 1986): 139-40.

30. Vigen Guroian. *Incarnate Love: Essays in Orthodox Ethics.* Notre Dame, IN: University of Notre Dame Press, 1989), p. 159.

31. Rose, p. 149.

32.   Guroian, p. 71.

33.   Frank Schaeffer. *Dancing Alone: The Quest for Orthodox Faith in the Age of False Religions.* (Brookline, MA: Holy Cross Orthodox Press, 1994), p. 301.

34.   Schaeffer, pp. 299-300.

Ch. 5

The Dance

1.   Quoted in Robert Payne's *The Fathers of the Eastern Church.* (New York: Dorset Press, 1989), p. 15.

2.   Metropolitan Anthony and Georges LeFebvre. *Courage to Pray.* (Crestwood, NY: St. Vladimir's Seminary Press, 1984), pp. 32-33.

3.   Monk Damascene Christensen. *Not of This World: The Life and Teachings of Fr. Seraphim Rose.* (Forestville, CA: Fr. Seraphim Rose Foundation, 1993), p. 200.

4.   Anthony M. Coniaris. *Discovering God Through the Daily Practice of His Presence.* (Minneapolis, MN: Light and Life Publishing, 1989), p. 18.

5.   Christensen, p. 931.

6.   John Climacus. *The Ladder of Divine Ascent.* Translated by Colm Luibheid and Norman Russell. (Ramsey, NJ: Paulist Press, 1982), p. 132.

7.   Thomas Merton. *New Seeds of Contemplation.* (New York: New Directions Publishing, 1972), pp. 296-7.

About the Author

David Beck has undergraduate degrees in English and in Sociology and a graduate degree in English. He is a Senior Lecturer for the English Department at Indiana University (at Indianapolis). He completed the St. Stephen's three-year program (Antiochian Diocese) and earned their Certificate in Orthodox Theology. A sub-deacon at Saints Constantine and Elena Romanian Orthodox Church in Indianapolis, he is married and has two children.

Made in the USA
Monee, IL
24 August 2021